"This volume, written by systemic therapy integration experts, is an essential guide for clinical supervisors interested in building their competency in IST. Providing both a clear conceptual framework as well as step-by-step guidelines, The Integrative Systemic Therapy Approach to Supervision, is roadmap to customize treatment to help supervisees meet the needs of their diverse individual, couple, and family systems."

Eli A. Karam, PhD, *LMFT, professor, University of Louisville, Kent School of Social Work & Family Science, AAMFT Clinical Training Award Recipient, Host/ Co-Executive Producer – The AAMFT Podcast*

"The authors have been admirably successful in achieving their goal of making IST supervision accessible to practitioners from a wide range of professional disciplines and levels of experience. Readers are bound to discover useful examples, whether their goals are simple curiosity or more ambitious levels of integrative supervision. Highly recommended!"

Thomas Todd, PhD, *Co-editor of* The Complete Systemic Supervisor

"I recommend this book to novices and experts alike. Using IST, the authors walk clinicians through unique ways to integrate the best interventions of various models of therapy. The material is presented in a clear, supportive language, with clinical examples to facilitate trainee competencies and growth."

Mudita Rastogi, PhD, *clinical professor and department chair, The Family Institute at Northwestern University*

Integrative Systemic Supervision

This book provides a comprehensive guide to applying Integrative Systemic Therapy (IST) principles in clinical supervision and training. It offers a solution to the challenges therapists face when integrating diverse therapeutic models.

In today's clinical practice, training based on single models is insufficient, and many therapists struggle to combine conflicting approaches. This book presents a theory-driven, hands-on method for supervisors to help therapists bridge these gaps and master integrative therapy from a systemic perspective. The first half focuses on IST supervision methods within cultural contexts, while the second half explores the development of both IST supervisors and therapists, with practical, real-world supervision examples throughout.

Invaluable to supervisors in marriage and family therapy, counseling, clinical psychology, and social work, the book equips readers with essential tools to enhance their supervision practice and expand their expertise in integrative therapy.

Yaliu He, PhD, LMFT, is an associate professor in Marriage and Family Therapy at Iona University. She is an AAMFT Approved Supervisor.

Nathan Hardy, PhD, LMFT, is an associate professor of Marriage and Family Therapy and the MFT Program Coordinator at Oklahoma State University. He is an AAMFT Approved Supervisor.

Adam Fisher, PhD, ABPP, is an associate clinical professor at Brigham Young University. He is an AASECT certified sex therapist, and a certified group psychotherapist. He is also a clinical lecturer at Northwestern University.

Neil Venketramen, LMFT, serves as a clinical lecturer and the Assistant Director for Clinical Training and Supervision at The Family Institute at Northwestern University. He is an AAMFT Approved Supervisor.

The Family Institute Series: Clinical Applications of the Integrative Systemic Therapy (IST) Model

Series editors: Anthony L. Chambers, Douglas C. Breunlin, William P. Russell, and Jay Lawrence Lebow

The Family Institute Series: Clinical Applications of the Integrative Systemic Therapy (IST) Model focuses on elaborating the theory and practice of Integrative Systemic Therapy (IST) and its application to various populations and contexts. Embracing empiricism, diversity, and creativity, the series distills the complex landscape of psychotherapy into clinician friendly guidelines and strategies useful to all practitioners and students in psychology, marriage and family therapy, counseling and the other mental health professions.

Titles in the series:

Integrative Systemic Therapy in Practice: A Clinician's Handbook
William P. Russell, Douglas C. Breunlin, and Bahareh Sahebi

Integrative Systemic Supervision: Training Therapists to Work with Individuals, Couples, and Families
Yaliu He, Nathan Hardy, Adam Fisher, and Neil Venketramen

Integrative Systemic Supervision

Training Therapists to Work with Individuals, Couples, and Families

Yaliu He, Nathan Hardy, Adam Fisher
and Neil Venketramen

Routledge
Taylor & Francis Group

NEW YORK AND LONDON

First published 2026
by Routledge
605 Third Avenue, New York, NY 10158

and by Routledge
4 Park Square, Milton Park, Abingdon, Oxon OX14 4RN

Routledge is an imprint of the Taylor & Francis Group, an informa business

Library of Congress Cataloging-in-Publication Data
A catalog record for this title has been requested

ISBN: 978-0-367-69520-0 (hbk)
ISBN: 978-0-367-70544-2 (pbk)
ISBN: 978-1-003-14684-1 (ebk)

DOI: 10.4324/9781003146841

Typeset in Sabon
by Taylor & Francis Books

Contents

Figures

Credit List

We would like to acknowledge Taylor & Francis Group, John Wiley & Sons, and the American Psychological Association for granting us permission to use figures from their existing publications.

Acknowledgments

The completion of this book occurred within a historical and ecological context. Since our supervision book is based on Integrative Systemic Therapy (IST), we would like to acknowledge the foundational work accomplished by the IST developers and contributors, including Bill Pinsof, Doug Breunlin, Bill Russell, Jay Lebow, Anthony Chambers, and Cheryl Rampage. The developers' collaboration over 30 years—rooted in their clinical, teaching, research, and training experience—has formed the key components and operational guidelines of IST. More importantly, the institution where they worked together, The Family Institute at Northwestern University, shared their vision for integrative systemic training and practice, providing instrumental support in integrating IST into the teaching of their prominent master's and postdoctoral training programs. It was there that we learned about IST from the original developers, opening a door to a new world where we discovered innovative ways of conceptualization and endless possibilities for growth as clinicians. We continued collaborating with the developers on IST after becoming faculty members and supervisors in different graduate training programs, resulting in several peer-reviewed journal articles, conference presentations, and now this book. We would like to express our immense gratitude to them and to all the individuals, including clients and students, who have contributed to IST.

Each of us works in different higher education institutions across various geographic locations in the United States. We have gained significant teaching and supervision experience at these institutions, which has solidified our thoughts on training that is both integrative and systemic. We want to thank our students, colleagues, and universities for their input and support. In particular, the opportunity to work with a diverse body of graduate students and their clients has enriched our discussions on the impact of culture on supervision and clinical practice.

We appreciate the thorough feedback from the editors of *The Family Institute Series: Clinical Application of the Integrative Systemic Therapy Model*, Anthony Chambers, Jay Lebow, Bill Russell, and Doug Breunlin. Their instrumental feedback throughout the process has strengthened our writing. A special thank you goes to Bahareh Sahebi, who has generously provided advice and guidance for the last chapter of the book. We also thank Kristin Patch, who diligently formatted the book, and our Routledge Editor, Julia Giordano, for her valuable and patient guidance.

Finally, we appreciate the important people in our lives who selflessly support our ambitions and efforts for this book: Yonghua He, Megan Hardy, Natalie Fisher, and Denise Venketramen. They are true inspirations and keep us going.

Preface

This book, *Integrative Systemic Supervision*, applies the principles of Integrative Systemic Therapy (IST) to the practice of clinical supervision and training. It presents supervisors with a theoretically grounded yet practical approach to strengthen therapists' capability to integrate concepts and interventions from various individual, couple, and family therapy models. This is the second book in Routledge's *The Family Institute Series: Clinical Applications of the Integrative Systemic Therapy Model*, following the publication of *Integrative Systemic Therapy in Practice: A Clinician's Handbook* (Russell et al., 2023). It builds on both the IST handbook and the original IST book, *Integrative Systemic Therapy: Metaframeworks for Problem Solving with Individuals, Couples, and Families* (Pinsof et al., 2018).

IST is a multi-theoretical and multisystemic perspective that provides a structure to organize and integrate concepts and interventions from various therapy models while attending to common factors. It offers therapists a solid foundation to utilize different concepts and interventions when working with families, couples, and individuals. The approach addresses a broad variety of presenting concerns and situations and can be applied across treatment modalities (individual, couple, and family therapy), mental health disciplines (marriage and family therapy, psychology, and social work), and diverse client populations across cultures.

The IST approach to supervision is beneficial for supervisors and therapists at various developmental stages and pathways, particularly if they share an interest in integration. It offers supervisors a comprehensive framework for working with therapists whose preferred models differ from their own. Supervisors with expertise in a single model, common factors, or another integrative approach can utilize tools from IST supervision to complement their skills. Additionally, it provides a structure to cultivate cultural humility, self-development, and supervisory relationships by attending to systemic factors including organization, development, culture, gender, spirituality, biology, and the mind.

Chapter 1 provides an overview of IST, especially focusing on the IST essence diagram and blueprint, using a vignette to guide readers through each step of their clinical applications. Chapter 2 defines the goals, structures, and roles of the supervisory relationship, and establishes a theoretical foundation for the approach. Chapter 3 explains the specific methods of using IST's essence diagram, blueprint, and guidelines to conduct IST supervision, illustrating key concepts with supervision vignettes. Chapter 4 discusses other important supervision topics, such as the use of technology, ethical and legal issues, risk management, and the evaluation of supervision outcomes. Chapter 5 focuses on the development of an IST supervisor by encouraging supervisors to consider their own unique backgrounds, the pathways of their growth and learning, and their current self-of-the-supervisor issues. A few supervision vignettes demonstrate supervisory challenges, interventions, and supervisor growth using IST tools. Parallel to their own development in IST supervision, supervisors play a crucial role in helping therapists develop the knowledge, skills, and personal growth necessary to become proficient in IST. Chapter 6 addresses various aspects of supervision that deal directly with therapists' development and roles in therapy, such as identifying the IST competencies that therapists must acquire and exploring the person of the therapist. Chapter 7 discusses IST training for therapists in different mental health professions with an emphasis on supervision that occurs in the context of graduate degree programs. The chapter discusses curricular elements that support the learning of IST and showcases an IST-centered curriculum that complements IST supervision.

Contributors

Yaliu He , PhD, LMFT, is an associate professor in the Department of Marriage and Family Therapy at Iona University. She has a deep passion for psychotherapy training, research, and clinical practice. She primarily trains clinicians using the Integrative Systemic Therapy (IST) perspective, a multi-theoretical, multi-systemic, and empirically informed approach that abstracts concepts and interventions from various therapies to facilitate effective changes for clients. She has published peer-reviewed articles and presented at national and international conferences on IST and IST supervision. Through the Relational Ethics Fellowship, she explores the intersection of relational ethics and multiculturalism in psychotherapy practice. Dr. He also conducts empirical research on interventions such as measurement feedback systems to improve psychotherapy engagement and outcomes, which have been published in top-tier journals such as *Psychological Assessment* and *Psychotherapy Research*. She served as an associate editor for *Family Process* from 2018 to 2023 and has been on the editorial board of the *Journal of Marital and Family Therapy* since 2021. Additionally, she is a clinical member and approved supervisor within American Association for Marriage and Family Therapy. https://orcid.org/0000-0003-0325-7787

Nathan R. Hardy , PhD, LMFT, is an associate professor of Marriage and Family Therapy and the MFT Program Coordinator at Oklahoma State University. His research focuses on improving marital functioning and preventing unnecessary divorce by examining services provided to couples, such as relationship education and couple therapy, and by identifying factors that promote marital quality and stability. He also seeks to improve overall training and practice in marriage and family therapy by exploring integrative systemic therapy, feedback-informed systemic therapy, and relational ethics in therapy. Dr. Hardy has been recognized for his contributions to the field, receiving the Relational Ethics in Therapy Fellowship. He is actively involved in professional organizations, serving as the Chair of the Family Therapy Section of the National Council on

Family Relations and as the past Secretary of the Couples and Intimate Relationships Interest Network of the American Association for Marriage and Family Therapy. He has authored numerous peer-reviewed publications and book chapters and is sought after as a presenter and trainer on topics related to couple therapy and MFT supervision and training. https://orcid.org/0000-0003-3199-6421

Adam Fisher , PhD, ABPP, is an associate clinical professor at Brigham Young University, with a joint appointment in the Department of Counseling Psychology and Special Education. He is also a clinical lecturer at Northwestern University. Dr. Fisher teaches courses in couple and family therapy and sex therapy, and mentors graduate students in their research projects on relationships and sexual health. Dr. Fisher works with couples, relationship challenges, and sexual health, including a focus on treating out-of-control sexual behavior (OCSB) in group therapy. Dr. Fisher is an AASECT certified sex therapist, a certified group psychotherapist, and board certified in couple and family psychology. He has served as a managing editor of the *Encyclopedia of Couple and Family Therapy*, and as the president of APA Division 43: The Society for Couple & Family Psychology (2024–2025). https://orcid.org/0009-0000-7898-6461

Neil Venketramen , LMFT, serves as a clinical lecturer and the Assistant Director for Clinical Training and Supervision at The Family Institute at Northwestern University. His professional focus is on the integration of cultural considerations into clinical practice, with an emphasis on the intersection between culture and clinical scholarship. As an Integrative Systemic clinician and supervisor, Mr. Venketramen specializes in working with couple relationships and advancing therapeutic practices through his research and teaching. His research explores the application of Integrative Systemic Therapy (IST) within clinical settings and investigates the influence of supervision practices on the professional development of clinicians. Mr. Venketramen is actively engaged in contributing to the field of marriage and family therapy through various presentations and workshops. He has presented locally on the effects of the COVID-19 pandemic on couple relationships and has conducted workshops focused on the principles of integrative supervision. Additionally, he has presented at international conferences on the cultural experiences of minority populations in therapy. A dedicated member of the American Association for Marriage and Family Therapy (AAMFT), Mr. Venketramen continues to make significant contributions to the academic and clinical advancement of marriage and family therapy through his leadership in supervision and training.

Chapter 1

Snapshot of Integrative Systemic Therapy

In the last two decades, the field of systemic therapy has been through a major shift. Therapists used to have a shared belief in systemic theory and treating the whole family together in therapy. Nowadays, many therapists learn and adopt specific therapy models that emphasize their advantages over other models and only work with a subsystem of a family (e.g., the parental subsystem). Although it is beneficial to train therapists in particular theoretical models, the limitations of practicing singular models are well recognized. For example, practicing specific models leads to a narrow conceptualization of the problem and solutions. It may miss the opportunities that other ways of conceptualizing and intervening benefit certain clients. Single models also limit the therapist's ability to work with a diverse body of clients and a broad range of presenting issues because their chosen approaches may not be effective for everyone (Castonguay et al., 2015). Despite the tendency to train in specific models, in actual practice, most therapists report they integrate different therapy methods rather than being committed to practicing one specific model (Orlinsky & Rønnestad, 2005). There is evidence the field is moving towards shared common principles instead of focusing on which model is better than the others (Wampler et al., 2019). Thus, it is extremely valuable to train therapists to practice an integrative approach that provides a comprehensive, theoretical perspective and can cut across different models. Better treatment effectiveness and alignment for clients is expected using an integrative approach because therapists are equipped with an overarching therapy guide while being open to learning various therapy concepts and techniques. Therapists are likely to have a broader range of clientele, more tools to handle different client concerns, lower burnout rates, and a more satisfying career.

To meet this need for theoretical integration in systemic therapy, Integrative Systemic Therapy (IST) creates a meta-theoretical perspective, grounded in systemic theory and integration, which transcends models in individual, couple, and family therapy (Pinsof et al., 2018). The goal of IST is to cultivate systemic training and integrative practice for twenty-first-century therapists. IST, which builds on the earlier integrative

DOI: 10.4324/9781003146841-1

models of William M. Pinsof (Pinsof, 1995) and Douglas C. Breunlin (Breunlin et al., 1992), was developed by Pinsof and Breunlin along with their colleagues William P. Russell, Jay L. Lebow, Cheryl Rampage, and Anthony L. Chambers at The Family Institute at Northwestern University. The approach is based on their more than 30 years of clinical practice, research, and training at the Master of Science in Marriage and Family Therapy (MSMFT) program at Northwestern University. The first IST book was published in English in 2018 (Pinsof et al., 2018) and translated to Mandarin in 2023. The current supervision book is the second book in Routledge's The Family Institute Series: Clinical Applications of Integrative Systemic Therapy. It follows the publication of the IST handbook (Russell et al., 2023), which is being translated in Mandarin and Italian.

IST Essence Diagram and IST Blueprint

IST provides a set of problem-solving steps derived from its theoretical pillars, core concepts, and therapy guidelines. They are thoroughly discussed in the 2018 and 2023 books mentioned above. We provide a brief overview of some core concepts in this chapter. If you are already familiar with IST, you can skip this chapter and go directly to Chapter 2.

IST's problem-solving steps are depicted in a flowchart called the essence diagram (please see Figure 1.1).

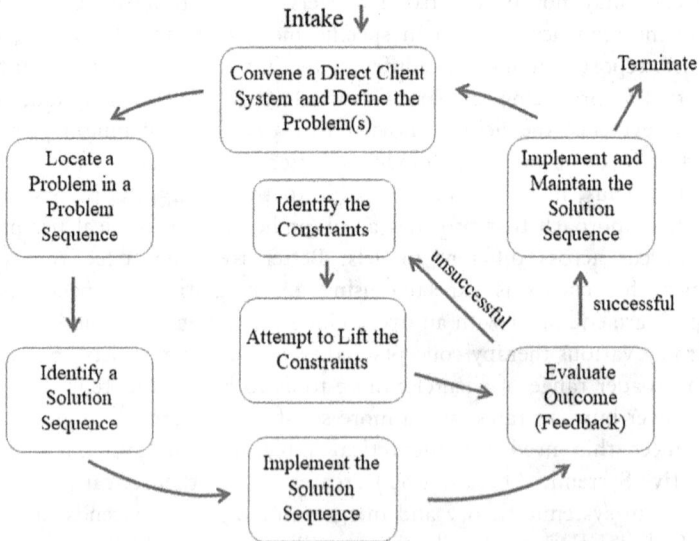

Figure 1.1 Essence Diagram of Problem-Solving in IST
Source: Russell et al., 2016, p. 531.

The essence of IST captures the problem-solving tasks of the therapy process; the blueprint in IST is used to operate the steps of essence while maintaining a good alliance with clients. Each step involves a complex and collaborative conversation guided by the therapy blueprint. The blueprint (see Figure 1.2) in IST addresses the process by which therapists make decisions about how to accomplish the essence steps and maintain a therapeutic alliance. This process governs what to do at any given moment of therapy as well as larger arcs of case conceptualization and planning. The blueprint describes the therapist's recursive process of hypothesizing, planning, conversing (intervening), and incorporating feedback at any given moment of therapy. This involves hypothesizing about the problem sequences, solution sequences, and constraints, planning to employ clinical strategies from different therapy models to remove constraints, conducting interventive conversations that implement those strategies, and assessing clients' feedback and responsiveness to maintain or revise a hypothesis.

IST utilizes a matrix (see Figure 1.3) that organizes strategies of interventions into planning metaframeworks (action, meaning/emotion, biobehavioral, family-of-origin, internal representation, and self) and contexts of therapy (family/community, couple/co-parent, and individual; Pinsof et al., 2018). The matrix offers a practical integration tool that guides the decision of how to draw clinical interventions and techniques from many different therapy models. Based on IST's cost-effective principle, therapists usually begin with a focus on the here and now with action-oriented strategies and progressively move down the matrix to dig deep into interactional patterns and individuals' internal issues (e.g., self-psychology or internal representation) when the action-oriented strategies do not work (see Figure 1.3).

There are other noteworthy guidelines of IST. The failure-driven principle frees the therapist or the client from having to "get it right" the first time. It allows the therapist and clients to embrace failure as a source of helpful feedback in therapy and in their personal life. Therapists usually tell clients that the tasks they agree on in therapy or outside of therapy (e.g., homework) are experiments. If the experiments are not successful, the therapist and the client work together to identify the constraints which prevent them from being successful and, if necessary, develop a new experiment (Pinsof et al., 2018). Another IST principle is the alliance priority principle. Drawing

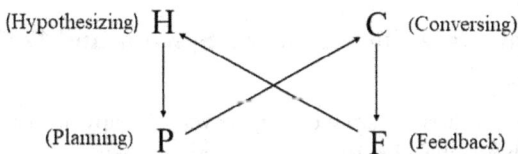

(Hypothesizing) H   C (Conversing)

(Planning) P   F (Feedback)

Figure 1.2 The Blueprint in IST
Source: Breunlin et al., 2011, p. 300.

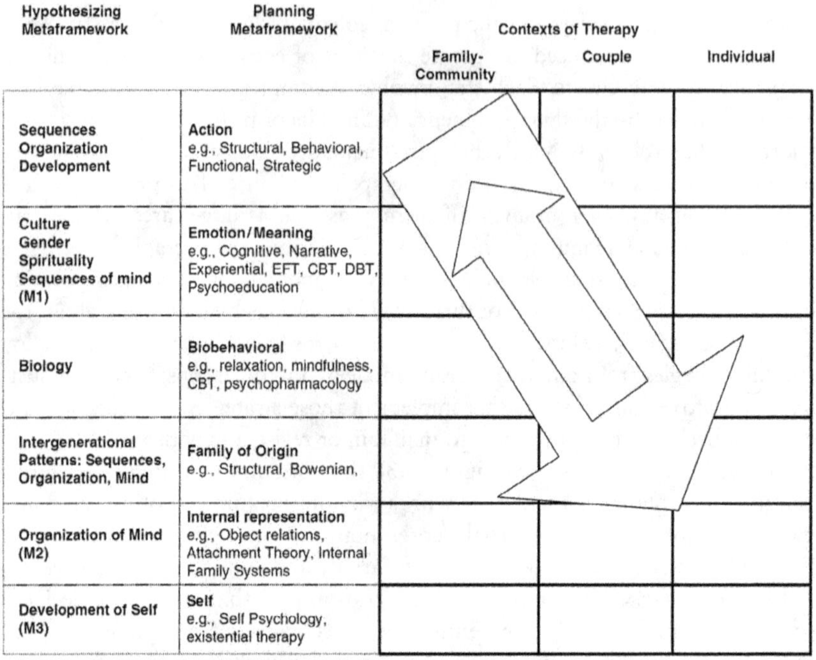

Hypothesizing Metaframework	Planning Metaframework	Contexts of Therapy		
		Family-Community	Couple	Individual
Sequences Organization Development	**Action** e.g., Structural, Behavioral, Functional, Strategic			
Culture Gender Spirituality Sequences of mind (M1)	**Emotion/Meaning** e.g., Cognitive, Narrative, Experiential, EFT, CBT, DBT, Psychoeducation			
Biology	**Biobehavioral** e.g., relaxation, mindfulness, CBT, psychopharmacology			
Intergenerational Patterns: Sequences, Organization, Mind	**Family of Origin** e.g., Structural, Bowenian,			
Organization of Mind (M2)	**Internal representation** e.g., Object relations, Attachment Theory, Internal Family Systems			
Development of Self (M3)	**Self** e.g., Self Psychology, existential therapy			

Figure 1.3 IST Planning Matrix
Source: Breunlin et al., 2011, p. 318

from the common factors approach, therapists are asked to prioritize therapeutic alliance over any other plans or actions, unless doing so compromises the integrity or effectiveness of therapy. Assessing, maintaining, and repairing the therapeutic alliance is an ongoing task in therapy.

The problem-solving steps of the essence diagram comprise a complex and recursive process. At each step, it involves a fair amount of back and forth in conversation based on the therapist's judgment and the clients' feedback. Furthermore, the conversations in IST are planful, but also improvisational and unique to the specific therapist and clients. The vignettes and associated dialogues included in this chapter are only examples and, consistent with equifinality, there are multiple conversations that can accomplish the essence tasks.

Step 1: Convene a Direct Client System and Define the Problem(s)

The purpose of a first session of any psychotherapy is usually gathering information about the client(s), understanding their concerns, and establishing a therapeutic contract. Similarly, in the essence diagram, the first step is to identify a direct client system and define the problem.

Client System   **Therapist System**

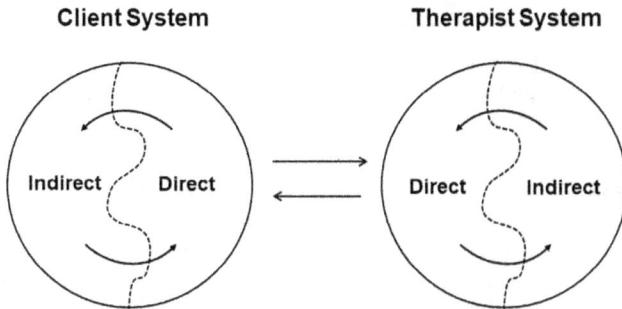

Indirect   Direct   Direct   Indirect

Figure 1.4 The Therapy System
Source: Pinsof et al., 2018, p. 46

Pinsof and colleagues designated people who may contribute to the maintenance and/or resolution of the presenting problem as *the client system* in IST (Pinsof et al., 2018). People in the client system may or may not be present at therapy. To help the therapist make pragmatic decisions about which family members to participate in therapy, the client system is divided into the direct client system and the indirect client system (Pinsof et al., 2018; see Figure 1.4). The *direct client system* refers to the group of people who attend therapy at any given session (Pinsof et al., 2018). The *indirect client system* is another group that may influence therapy and contribute to the maintenance and resolution of the problem but is not directly involved in therapy (Pinsof et al., 2018). Although people in the indirect client system do not participate in therapy, therapy may have a significant impact on their lives (e.g., the spouse of an individual seeking therapy who is discussing divorce) and the indirect client system can have significant impact on the therapy (e.g., they do not support the direct system's goal for therapy). The benefit of considering the indirect client systems is that the therapist is determining who may impact the maintenance or the resolution of the problem outside of therapy and how their lives may be potentially impacted by therapy outcomes. IST has an interpersonal guideline that therapists should prioritize working within a relational context directly involving multiple people in the client system rather than an individual client unless the client strongly insists on being seen individually or safety concerns arise. The rationale is that having the family system be present at therapy provides opportunities for the therapist to directly observe their interaction patterns and gather information from multiple people's perspectives so the therapist can understand and intervene in the problem sequence with the system.

Similarly, the therapist system consists of the direct therapist system which is the therapist conducting the sessions, and the indirect therapist system that includes people who may be involved with the care of the client system (including supervisors, other supervisees, other therapists who worked with the client system in the past, psychiatrists, primary care doctors, school personnel, social workers, and case manager, etc.). In IST, the therapist is responsible for collaborating with the people in the indirect therapist system to provide coherent and holistic treatment for the client system.

The initial contact between a therapist and a client usually begins with the first phone call. During this phone call, the therapist starts gathering information about clients' concerns and building an early therapeutic alliance. Through the information collected from clients, the therapist makes an initial hypothesis about what the problem is and who may be suitable to join therapy. The selection of the direct client system may depend on the therapist's hypothesis regarding the most influential members of the family who contribute to the problem and the family members' willingness and availability.

Now we will illustrate the essence diagram step by step using a vignette. In the following vignette, one partner contacted the therapist and wanted to do couple therapy. Through asking the caller several questions around the client's primary concern, the therapist decided who was in the direct client system.

Joshua, a Filipino American male in his early 40s, called the therapist to schedule an appointment for couple therapy in an outpatient setting. The therapist was an Asian female in her 30s. Joshua reported having constant arguments with his wife, Andrea, who was two years younger than him. She was from the Philippines as well. Joshua mentioned that they had two adolescent boys, 12-year-old Benjamin and 15-year-old Alexander. After a brief self-introduction, the therapist began identifying the problem.

THERAPIST: Could you please tell me about your primary reason for coming to therapy?

JOSHUA: My marriage needs some work. Andrea and I have been married for 17 years. Over time we are less connected with each other as we raised our kids. Andrea has some specific concerns, but I don't want to speak for her. She will share with you when you meet.

THERAPIST: If I understand correctly, you would like to strengthen your relationship, so you feel more emotionally connected with Andrea. Is that correct?

JOSHUA: Yes, that's right.

THERAPIST: Is your primary concern around your relationship as a couple? In addition to your marriage, do you have any other concerns? How are your children doing?

JOSHUA: Our primary goal is to work on our relationship. However, I noticed my kids were noticeably quiet at home. I am not sure if that's just a teenage thing or something else is going on. My kids saw me and Andrea arguing several times. They looked scared and tried to stop our argument. Andrea and I did not want them to worry about us, so we headed to our bedroom and shut the door.

THERAPIST: Did you talk to Benjamin and Alexander about your argument?

JOSHUA: No, we did not. In Asian culture, people tend to avoid conflicts. I don't know how to have open discussions with them although it seems they are worried about us. Plus, it is hard to explain to them about our problems which will get them more worried. I hope we can figure it out by ourselves.

THERAPIST: I see. Do they know you are seeking couple therapy?

JOSHUA: No, I don't want them to know. My wife and I are very private. It took us a long time to even decide to go to couple therapy. We do not want to get our kids involved and let them worry about us.

THERAPIST: Understood. Is there anyone else you think is important to address the concern you and your wife have?

JOSHUA: Maybe my parents who still live in the Philippines? One of our arguments is that Andrea thought I sent too much money back home to support them. But they are far away, so I guess they are not interested in becoming part of our therapy and of course I do not want them to know our marital issues now.

THERAPIST: I understand your concern. Let's just invite you and your wife to attend therapy at this moment. If things change, we can always revisit whether inviting your children or parents would be helpful.

JOSHUA: Sounds good.

In the first phone call, the therapist sensed Joshua had some hesitations seeking psychotherapy through his tone of voice and the fact that it took a long time for them to initiate couple therapy. Using the blueprint, the therapist hypothesized that Benjamin and Alexander might be impacted by their marital problem and the couple might disagree about their financial decision-making pertaining to supporting Joshua's parents. Because Joshua did not want anyone else to know they are seeking couple therapy, the therapist hypothesized it might be related to the mental health stigma in his culture or his family. Based on these initial hypotheses as well as Joshua's stated goals and preferences, the therapist planned to invite Joshua and Andrea to attend therapy while keeping their children and Joshua's parents in the indirect client system for now. The therapist still left open the possibility of inviting them later to therapy if needed. As Joshua only shared his perspective about the problem, the therapist planned to work with the couple to define the problem in the first session.

Joshua and Andrea came to therapy for the first session. They both looked friendly, and Joshua seemed shy. They shook hands and the therapist introduced herself. Andrea said it was her first time attending therapy and asked about the therapist's therapy method. It is common for clients to ask the therapist what method is used and how effective it is. The therapist used this opportunity to introduce IST and build their therapeutic alliance by seeking alignment on the goals and tasks of therapy. The therapist also introduced the four-session couple therapy assessment which is an optional assessment method developed by Chambers (2012) that is compatible with IST for couples (also see Pinsof et al., 2018, chapter 10). Many other couple therapy models use a four-session therapy assessment module as well, including a conjoint session, two individual sessions with each partner, and a conjoint feedback session at the end. The therapist hypothesized that they might have some doubts about therapy or simply be unfamiliar with it. She planned to ask them for feedback about their first session later.

THERAPIST: That is a great question. The therapeutic approach I use is Integrative Systemic Therapy. As a systemic therapist, I view the issues clients bring up as interaction patterns involving multiple people. Most often, a relational problem or even an individual problem is not one person's fault. As we are in relationships, the problem often occurs in the way people interact with each other. In this case, multiple people participate and play a role. My job is to help clients identify problematic interactive patterns and change the way people behave, think, or feel during their interactions to resolve the issue. I see the first four sessions as the assessment phase. Today is the first conjoint session and I will collect information about your relationship and identify the problem we will be working on. In the next two sessions, I will interview each of you individually to understand your individual adjustment and family of origin. In the fourth session, I will provide feedback regarding the strengths and potential issues in your relationship and seek your agreement to work on some specific goals. As Joshua showed some concerns regarding Benjamin and Alexander and he mentioned you had a disagreement about the financial support for his parents in the Philippines, we will also discuss if it is necessary to involve them in therapy later. Does that sound like a plan?

Andrea and Joshua nodded their heads and did not have further questions.

THERAPIST: Okay. Great. Let's get started.

The therapist asked the couple a few questions regarding their marriage such as marital history as well as their individual functioning and family relationships (parent-child relationships). Joshua and Andrea met at a mutual friend's party 17 years ago and began dating right away. Joshua was a first-generation Filipino American and Andrea was a second-generation Filipino American. Joshua was a math teacher in an elementary school and Andrea was an accountant in a local food company. When asked what brought each of them to therapy, Andrea said that she wanted to repair the trust in their relationship while Joshua wanted to address the lack of effort they have put into their relationship since having kids.

Andrea shared her concerns regarding Joshua's previous affair with a coworker. Joshua looked frustrated hearing it. He admitted that a year ago he had lunch with a female coworker and one time they kissed. He immediately told Andrea about it and apologized. Then he stopped seeing the coworker. Joshua could not understand why they had to talk about it again. He wanted to focus on the lack of connection in their relationship now. Hearing this, Andrea looked frustrated. Turning attention to Joshua's concern, the therapist asked Joshua when he felt less connected to Andrea. Joshua said that it began after they had kids as they spent less time together and it got exacerbated in the last two years since Andrea changed jobs. He thought Andrea spent too much time at work and with their children, and he felt he was being ignored.

The problems that the partners identified looked different. Joshua was concerned about their lack of connection and Andrea was worried about lack of trust. The therapist validated their feelings and thoughts and decided to collect more information in the individual sessions to find the problem in a problem sequence.

Step 2: Locate a Problem in a Problem Sequence

Corresponding to the sequence pillar, one important task for the therapist is to locate the client's presenting concerns within a problem sequence. The therapist needs to ask a series of questions aimed at what typically happens before, during, and after the presenting issue or conflict so they can understand the interactive sequence around the problem.

In individual sessions, the therapist asked them each about their different views on the importance of talking about the affair because the therapist hypothesized this discrepancy may be part of their problem sequence. Joshua admitted that he felt ashamed of talking about the affair as he did not want to face his mistake. Andrea mentioned that she could not trust him since the affair and had distanced herself from him emotionally and sexually even more. Given that having kids seemed to be a turning point of their relationship satisfaction, the therapist asked about how their relationship was before their children's birth. They reported high satisfaction prior to entering parenthood, which confirmed the therapist's hypothesis. Andrea said that she changed to a part-time job to take care of her children. Since her children entered adolescence, Andrea went back to a full-time job to pursue her career goals. They now agreed with the fact that Andrea spent lots of time with the kids when they were young. Joshua felt lonely but felt embarrassed to tell Andrea. After Andrea switched to a full-time job two years ago, Joshua felt even more so and that is partially why he sought attention from his coworker. The therapist hypothesized the problem sequence being that important, unspoken feelings about their adjustment after the children's birth kept them from engaging with each other, which contributed to the occurrence of the affair and more distance and mistrust.

Although Joshua believed that his apology for the affair was enough, Andrea needed a longer time to recover from the betrayal. Reflected in their current interaction, Andrea got angry when she mentioned the affair during an argument, which made Joshua withdraw further. Therefore, the problem is not the childbirth or the affair, but the way Joshua and Andrea interacted with each other after the childbirth and the affair.

The therapist shared her hypothesis about the problem sequence with the couple in the fourth conjoint session and constantly observed their responses and asked them for feedback. The therapist pointed out that their concerns were different, but they were closely related, and both can be in the problem sequence. Hearing the hypothesized problem sequence, the couple realized that they each played a role in their lack of communication, trust, and connection. They agreed with the hypothesis and were willing to take a closer look at it. Based on the therapist's recommendation, they reached an agreement to work on a common goal: rebuild their trust and intimacy.

Step 3: Identify a Solution Sequence

After reaching an agreement about a problem sequence with clients, the next step is to generate a solution sequence that replaces part or all the problem sequences. When the problem sequence is clearly identified and clients agree with it, the therapist will facilitate a conversation regarding what the clients can do to solve their problem. This conversation can be brought up by the therapist with a question: "What are the things each of you can do differently to prevent the escalation of the problem?" The process of finding a solution sequence is collaborative. The therapist invites the client to think about a solution sequence. Unlike therapy approaches that discourage therapists from offering their opinions, the IST therapist shares their own thoughts about the clients' concerns and offers suggestions for solution sequence. However, they need to do this in a collaborative way that respects the client's autonomy and incorporates their feedback.

During the next two sessions, the therapist and the couple brainstormed about a potential solution sequence. Using the development hypothesizing metaframeworks, the therapist referenced research studies to normalize the decline of couple satisfaction following the birth of the first child. The therapist validated Joshua's regret and reluctance to talk about the affair. At the same time, the therapist insisted that it needed to be discussed in therapy because it is part of the problem sequence. The therapist leveraged Joshua's high commitment to the marriage, which the therapist recalled from the information collected in the individual session. This encouraged Joshua to be more open to reflecting on his participation in the affair.

THERAPIST: As I understand it, this problem sequence began when you transitioned to parenthood, which, according to research, is a family life stage where many couples struggle with their marital relationship. New parents have less time for each other when they adjust to the role. Joshua, you felt left out when Andrea spent so much of her energy working and taking care of the kids. Andrea, I understand that you felt stressed too because you also had to work. Because there were not sufficient communications about what you were experiencing, you felt distanced from each other, and intimacy declined. Your relationship declined further after Andrea went back to a full-time job and then the affair happened. The affair led to mistrust and increased your conflict, which might cause your children to worry about you. My suspicion is that you have not thoroughly discussed the impact of the affair.

Both Joshua and Andrea agreed with the therapist's hypothesis.

THERAPIST: How about what each of you could have done differently when these events occurred? I know these things are in the past, but you can always learn from what happened and prevent it from happening again in the future. Let's start with what can be changed after your children are born.

ANDREA: If he told me that he felt lonely while I was busy with work and childcare, I could give him more attention and time. I felt alone too. Because of my traditional values, I thought women should take the primary responsibility of taking care of the kids. That's what I did. However, along the way, I felt exhausted and wished he could help.

JOSHUA: Yeah, I agree with Andrea. But somehow it never came to my mind to tell her. Reflecting, I just did not feel comfortable telling her.

THERAPIST: It seems at that time both of you felt alone and wanted more support, but you did not communicate with your partner. Instead, you struggled alone.

JOSHUA: Yes, that's right. I felt ashamed to tell Andrea about my real feelings.

ANDREA: I agree. I inherited the gender roles from my family as my mother was the caregiver and my dad was the breadwinner. I did not anticipate Joshua could play a more active role as a father. Although I did not ask, I felt resentful of being the primary caregiver. We never talked about how to divide the tasks of being parents.

THERAPIST: You found a solution sequence. That is to communicate with each other in real time about your true feelings and concerns instead of keeping things to yourself. Did I understand it correctly? If that is right, does it apply to your relationship now? Can it be a solution sequence for resolving your conflicts and making a connection now?

Joshua and Andrea both agreed that this solution sequence would work for dealing with distance between them. They felt relieved that they understood their problem and at least knew what to work on.

Step 4: Implement the Solution Sequence

When the therapist and the client agree on a solution sequence, the therapist will encourage the clients to implement it either in therapy or outside of therapy. The therapist may ask or suggest when and how to do it while making sure the client understands this is an experiment and that they will talk later about how it goes.

After Joshua and Andrea agreed with the solution sequence, the therapist promoted direct communication between the couple to share their feelings, thoughts, and needs. The therapist decided to draw interventions from several behavioral couple therapy approaches as they are the most direct and cost-effective. The therapist asked the couple to each select a topic related to the problem sequence that they would like to discuss, and then assigned the couple to take turns to play the role of a speaker and an empathic responder. This exercise is introduced in multiple couple therapy models, called different names such as "listener-speaker exercise," "reflective listening exercise," and "emotional expressiveness exercise." Different from a problem-solving conversation, it helps the couple to express themselves and understand each other with the therapist's active coaching. Joshua wanted to talk about his loneliness and lack of sexual intimacy, and Andrea wanted to talk about the affair's impact on her. Because the therapist was concerned that Andrea would see Joshua's expression of loneliness as an excuse for his affair, the therapist explained to the couple that she would like Andrea to speak first. Joshua thought it was fair. After the purpose and procedure of this exercise was introduced, the couple faced each other, and Andrea began talking to Joshua.

Andrea told Joshua that she was shocked and felt traumatized after she learned about the affair. She said that she had trouble sleeping at night and kept wondering why Joshua betrayed her. It was shocking as she did not notice there was anything wrong with their relationship. She moved from scrutinizing herself for any mistake she might make to blaming Joshua for ruining their family. Then she found herself looking for issues to argue about, mostly criticizing Joshua for small mistakes he made, just to express her anger. When Andrea spoke, she was angry initially and later had tears, looking sad. There were times Andrea experienced intense emotions and began criticizing Joshua. The therapist interrupted Andrea, restated her role in the exercise, and provided soothing techniques for her to regulate her emotions. There were times Joshua wanted to defend himself. The therapist also interrupted him and brought him back to the listener role. Joshua repeated what Andrea said, but it was clear he did not fully understand it.

Step 5: Evaluate Outcome (Feedback)

Following the clients' first time implementing the solution sequence, the therapist immediately evaluates if it is successful by asking for the clients' feedback. The therapist asks what went well and what did not and discusses the reasons in either scenario. The first attempt may go well for some clients, and a set of solution sequences are sufficient to resolve the presenting concerns. In this case, the therapist compliments the clients' efforts and builds on the solution sequence with repetition and considers its impact on the problem sequence. In this case example, each partner will need opportunities to share their thoughts and feelings. Then therapy can skip steps 5 and 6 and go directly to step 7—implement and maintain the solution sequence—and move toward termination of therapy or on to another presenting concern.

It is common that the first attempt at implementation is unsuccessful. The client may not attempt the solution at all and report that they do not have time or skills, or they have other concerns. Other times the client attempts it and is not able to consistently implement it for a longer period. It is important for the therapist to validate the client's courage to act regardless of the outcome. Because the therapist framed it as an experiment earlier, the therapist tells the client to embrace failure and brainstorm what they can do next. Given that one of the common factors is to instill hope, the therapist keeps a positive outlook and encourages the client to try again.

As the therapist found Joshua having difficulty listening and responding empathically to Andrea's pain, the therapist paused the couple's dialogue and asked them what they thought about the process. Andrea said she tried hard to be vulnerable but did not feel Joshua put in enough effort. Feeling blamed, Joshua got frustrated and shut down. The therapist hypothesized that Andrea would be open to sharing her concerns and vulnerable feelings. However, because she had multiple attacks towards Joshua and Joshua seemed not to be able to listen with compassion, the first attempt of implementing the solution sequence was only partially successful. The next step was to identify the constraints.

Steps 6 and 7: Identify the Constraints and Attempt to Lift the Constraints

According to the constraint pillar, when the implementation of the solution sequence does not go well, the therapist helps the client explore the potential constraints. It usually begins with a question: "What prevents you from implementing the solution sequence?"

THERAPIST: Joshua, how were you feeling and what were you thinking when you listened to Andrea?

JOSHUA: I wanted to engage with her thoughts and feelings. However, my mind kept saying that it had already happened, so why can't she let it go. I apologized and I admitted it was a huge mistake. What else can I do? I felt helpless.

THERAPIST: Your reactions are normal. Human beings tend to develop counterarguments when they feel they are being attacked. I understand you have your thoughts and feelings about the affair as well, which you will have an opportunity to express later when you become the speaker. I appreciate your insights and awareness of what was going on in your mind. It seems the thought that both of you should move on and the feeling of helplessness kept you from listening to Andrea; is that correct?

JOSHUA: Yes, that's right.

THERAPIST: What else keeps you from being more emotionally empathic with her?

JOSHUA: (looking at the floor): It is painful to be reminded about my fault. You know. I felt deeply ashamed.

THERAPIST: I really appreciate that you shared your true thoughts and vulnerable feelings. Do you think they have something to do with gender roles and gender expression? For example, men are supposed to assume certain roles and express their emotions in a certain way?

JOSHUA: Yes, I believe so. In my culture, as an Asian man, you should not show feelings, at least not vulnerable feelings. It is a weakness. Men should be tough and never talk about feelings.

THERAPIST: Okay. Asking "What's the point of talking about the past if you cannot change it?" demonstrates a problem-solving belief. However, in a couple relationship, a lot of things cannot be easily solved. I think it has something to do with gender roles too.

ANDREA: Yes, he is indeed a problem-solver.

Using the gender hypothesizing metaframework, the therapist thought that part of the constraint was Joshua's "problem-solving" mind and his reluctance to show vulnerability due to gender roles in his culture. This conversation is an example of a therapist drawing from the emotion/meaning planning metaframework on the IST planning matrix (Figure 1.3). The therapist explored the emotion and meaning behind the gender roles within their respective cultural context and identity and how they constrain their current behaviors and couple interactions.

The therapist helped Joshua to understand that his way of gender expression prevented him from being connected with Andrea's pain. Joshua also realized that Andrea needed more reassurance through his verbal affirmation and consistent actions in helping with household chores. With the therapist's coaching, Andrea identified certain household chores she wanted Joshua to do, and Joshua was willing to do them. Having more practice with direct communication and empathic response in therapy, Joshua overcame his feeling of shame and received Andrea's forgiveness. The same exercise was used for Joshua to express his loneliness and for Andrea to respond empathically. Because Andrea witnessed Joshua's change in emotional expression and more active participation in household chores, Andrea was able to validate Joshua's feelings and apologized for ignoring him while she was busy with childcare and work.

Step 8: Implement and Maintain the Solution Sequence

As it takes time to shape a new behavior, the client needs time to consolidate their progress, especially applying the changes they make in therapy to their daily life. When the therapist determines that the client system can implement the positive changes more independently, they may decrease the frequency of therapy and work towards termination. If the client has new constraints, they will go back to step 5 and 6. If the client has a new goal, they may start all over from step 1—identifying a new problem.

With more communication practice in therapy and homework assigned outside of therapy (e.g., date night), Andrea and Joshua believed their relationship was stronger. They applied the same communication skills to conversations about financial assistance to Joshua's parents. With the therapist's coaching drawn from the culture hypothesizing metaframework, the couple understood there were cultural differences about taking care of elderly parents as Joshua immigrated to the US from a collectivist culture and Andrea grew up in the US culture which focuses on individualism. The therapist introduced new "problem-solving" skills and the couple negotiated what was acceptable to each of them and reached an agreement. With that, the therapist asked them to evaluate their treatment progress. The couple agreed that their initial goals were met but they expressed concern about their children. They thought their children might have been negatively impacted by the many arguments that occurred prior to the couple starting therapy. The therapist suggested that it would be beneficial to invite their children to therapy (become part of the direct client system) and restart the process of identifying a new goal.

As emphasized before, the steps of the IST essence are recursive. The therapist may go back to the previous step, responding to the client's feedback and their own reflections. For example, if the therapist realizes the hypothesis about the problem sequence is not accurate after the implementation of the solution sequence is unsuccessful, they will revisit step 2 and redefine the problem sequence. The presentation of the above case is not meant to suggest that therapy is as simple and straightforward as it looks. The therapist may make mistakes or need to reconsider the direction of therapy based on information or developments in the client system that were not previously considered. The complexity in human beings and their interactive dynamics with others justifies the need for theoretical integration. No one therapy model can capture such complexity, and the therapist can easily get lost. The IST blueprint is crucial because through the recursive process of hypothesizing, planning, conversing, and incorporating feedback, the therapist can feel more confident that they are making informed decisions at a given moment and over the course of therapy.

Conclusion

This chapter summarizes IST's two major conceptual tools for the conduct of integrative and systemic therapy: its problem-solving essence and its blueprint for therapy. If you are interested in learning more about IST, there are a number of other published works (e.g., Pinsof et al., 2018; Breunlin et al., 2011; Hardy et al., 2019; He et al., 2021; Pinsof et al., 2011, 2018; Russell & Breunlin, 2019; Russell et al., 2016; Russell et al., 2023). IST supervision, which is built on the concepts of IST explained in this chapter, will be the focus of the rest of this book.

References

Breunlin, D. C., Pinsof, W., & Russell, W. P. (2011). Integrative problem-centered metaframeworks therapy I: Core concepts and hypothesizing. *Family Process, 50* (3), 293–313. https://doi.org/10.1111/j.1545-5300.2011.01362.x.

Breunlin, D. C., Schwartz, R. C., & Mac Karrer, B. (1992). *Metaframeworks: Transcending the models of family therapy.* Jossey-Bass.

Castonguay, L. G., Eubanks, C. F., Goldfried, M. R., Muran, J. C., & Lutz, W. (2015). Research on psychotherapy integration: Building on the past, looking to the future. *Psychotherapy Research, 25*(3), 365–382. http://dx.doi.org/10.1080/10503307.2015.1014010.

Chambers, A. L. (2012). A systemically infused integrative model for conceptualizing couples' problems: The four-session evaluation. *Couple and Family Psychology: Research and Practice, 1*(1), 31–47. https://doi.org/10.1037/a0027505.

Hardy, N. R., Brosi, M. W., & Gallus, K. L. (2019). Integrative systemic therapy: Lessons on collaboration and training for the 21st century. *Journal of Marital and Family Therapy, 45*(2), 206–218. https://doi.org/10.1111/jmft.12332.

He, Y., Hardy, N., & Russell, W. (2021). Integrative systemic supervision: Promoting therapists' theoretical integration in systemic therapy. *Family Process, 61*(1), 58–75. https://doi.org/10.1111/famp.12667.

Orlinsky, D. E., & Rønnestad, M. H. (2005). *How psychotherapists develop: A study of therapeutic work and professional growth.* American Psychological Association.

Pinsof, W. M. (1995). *Integrative problem-centered therapy: A synthesis of family, individual, and biological therapies.* Basic Books.

Pinsof, W., Breunlin, D. C., Russell, W. P., & Lebow, J. (2011). Integrative problem-centered metaframeworks therapy II: Planning, conversing, and reading feedback. *Family Process, 50*(3), 314–336. https://doi.org/10.1111/j.1545-5300.2011.01361.x.

Pinsof, W. M., Breunlin, D. C., Russell, W. P., Lebow, J. L., Rampage, C., & Chambers, A. L. (2018). *Integrative systemic therapy: Metaframeworks for problem solving with individuals, couples, and families.* American Psychological Association.

Russell, W. P., & Breunlin, D. C. (2019). Transcending therapy models and managing complexity: Suggestions from integrative systemic therapy. *Family Process, 58* (3), 641–655. https://doi.org/10.1111/famp.12482.

Russell, W. P., Breunlin, D. C., & Sahebi, B. (2023). *Integrative systemic therapy in practice: A clinician's handbook*. Routledge.

Russell, W., Pinsof, W., Breunlin, D., & Lebow, J. (2016). Integrative problem-centered metaframeworks (IPCM) therapy. In T. Sexton, & J. Lebow (Eds.), *Handbook of family therapy* (4th ed., pp. 530–544). Routledge.

Wampler, K. S., Blow, A. J., McWey, L. M., Miller, R. B., & Wampler, R. S. (2019). The profession of couple, marital, and family therapy (CMFT): Defining ourselves and moving forward. *Journal of Marital and Family Therapy*, 45(1), 5–18. https://doi.org/10.1111/jmft.12294.

Chapter 2

What Is Integrative Systemic Supervision?

This chapter will provide an overview of the goals, structures, roles of the supervisor and the therapist, and expectations of IST supervision. It establishes a theoretical foundation for IST supervision before describing in detail how to conduct IST supervision in Chapter 3. In this book, to make the writing concise, the term "therapist" is used in a broad way to describe all supervisees at different stages who receive ongoing supervision from their clinical supervisors, including student therapists in training, postgraduate therapists in training, and licensed therapists who are more experienced. Clinical supervision, including IST supervision, occurs in various contexts, including graduate schools, postgraduate settings, and professional employment. The context of supervision will influence how supervisors are assigned and the duration of the supervisory relationship. Regardless of context, the purpose of the first supervision meeting involves reaching a consensus on goals and tasks of supervision, discussing confidentiality, ethics, and professionalism, and setting up an evaluation system to obtain feedback from the supervisor and the therapist.

This chapter begins with a supervision vignette that shows how the first IST supervision meeting may look in an academic program that does not primarily focus on training students to be IST therapists. The dialogue between the supervisor and the therapist reflects a process of introducing IST to therapists in the first meeting. Even though the faculty member works with the student in academic courses, it is important for them to form a supervisory relationship that differs from an instructor–student relationship.

Vignette: The First Supervision Meeting

Veronica, a 24-year-old second-year Latina student in a Marriage and Family Therapy master's program, received individual supervision from an IST supervisor. Veronica started her practicum at the program's clinic six months ago. In their first meeting, the supervisor asked Veronica about her knowledge and skills in therapy theories. Veronica said that she was still exploring which therapy theory fits her the best. The supervisor informed Veronica that she used an integrative systemic framework to conduct supervision. The supervisor clarified that

DOI: 10.4324/9781003146841-2

the ultimate goal is to promote the therapist's clinical competence defined by their specific field and support their short-term and long-term professional development. The IST framework serves as a theoretical foundation for the therapist to understand the general process of conducting systemic therapy through an integrative lens. It sets the stage for the therapist to integrate and apply concepts and techniques from various therapy models for their long-term development.

VERONICA: [looking confused]: I thought I should develop my expertise in one model before I dig deep into other models. Many students in my class have indicated their favorite approach. For example, Cathy really likes the Gottman couple therapy approach and wants to be certified as a Gottman method therapist. That is what we have been told in classes. I have not heard anything about integrative therapy yet.

It is common that therapists are told by their educators or previous supervisors to pick one therapy model first and to become good at it. The concept of integration is foreign to some students. Some therapists may misunderstand what integration is and confuse it with eclecticism which lacks a coherent theory that organizes therapy and guides decision-making. However, some therapists welcome the idea of integration and want to learn more. The supervisor needs to be prepared to explain integration and IST at the beginning of supervision so that the therapist is fully aware of how their supervision will be conducted and the rationale of it.

THE SUPERVISOR: Veronica, thanks for sharing your honest thoughts. Let's discuss this. As you pointed out, there may be two different training paths in integrative therapy: one is for therapists to become competent with one model and then expand to other models; the other approach is to train therapists in an integrative approach at the beginning and gradually teach them how to apply concepts and strategies from various therapy models and research in clinical work. Does that make sense?

VERONICA: Yes, I believe that's the case. I am familiar with the first method but have not heard about the second one.

THE SUPERVISOR: That is totally fine. Let us talk about their similarities and differences. What is your understanding about their differences?

VERONICA: The order is different. The first one is that you learn one thing first and learn more later. Then hopefully you integrate them. The second one is that you integrate models first before you learn specific models. It is just like one is from one to the whole and the other one is from the whole to one.

THE SUPERVISOR: That is a great summary. You are right. The order is different. What about their similarities?

VERONICA: Let me think. Although they are quite different, they share the same goal, which is to help therapists become good at multiple models, not just one. Is that right?

THE SUPERVISOR: That is correct. Do you think one is necessarily better than the other?

VERONICA: I don't know. I was always told to begin with one. So that's the only way I know. Can you explain more about the second approach?

THE SUPERVISOR: Sure. There are multiple methods for training an integrative therapist. The method I use, Integrative Systemic Therapy, is one of them. First, what do you know about integration?

VERONICA: Integration probably means that the therapist draws interventions from different therapy models and can work across multiple models.

THE SUPERVISOR: Great start. But how?

VERONICA: The therapist learns multiple therapy models and knows when to use which model with which client based on their knowledge and experience. Is that right?

THE SUPERVISOR: You're on the right track. Integration should help therapists decide which interventions to use. The question is just how those decisions are made. Therefore, integration should go beyond the level of integrating several different models or interventions. Integration is not collective or eclectic. Integration is not about selecting interventions from different models based on a clinician's instinct or experience. It is not to use one model with one client or a population and use a different model with another client or another population. Instead, integration should provide a theoretical conceptual framework consisting of coherent principles that organize therapy and guide decisions on the questions of what to do in therapy and when to do it. Therefore, the therapist's clinical decision is informed by fundamental principles and made with intention. It is important for the therapist to follow the principles, so they know what to do next when what they are doing does not work for the client. Does it make sense?

VERONICA: Yes, sort of. Can you give an example about what is and what is not integration?

THE SUPERVISOR: Sure. If talking about integrating a psychoanalytic approach with Bowenian therapy, it is relatively easy because they both emphasize the impact of one's childhood experiences/family of origin on individual development. Although psychoanalytic therapy is more individual-focused and Bowenian therapy is more family-focused, their similarities make it easy for therapists to conceptualize cases across these two approaches and utilize interventions from either of them with one case. In comparison, it is more difficult to integrate Bowenian therapy with CBT (cognitive behavioral therapy) as they have very different theoretical assumptions about the problem and the solution. Therapists can use both a genogram and behavioral activation with a case, but there is no theoretical connection between these two interventions. It is more likely that the therapist at one point feels a genogram can help and in the next session decides to try behavioral activation. There is no metatheory to guide the therapist's decision-making.

VERONICA: Okay, I hear you. You said that we need common ground to make decisions with what to do and which interventions to use. Yes, I do not want to use one model for every client. I see the value of being trained in an integrative approach. However, I think the first route is easier because I am worried as a therapist in training that I don't have enough knowledge and experience to learn a metatheory. I am afraid it is too complicated, and I will feel overwhelmed.

It is normal for therapists early in the training process to feel anxious about learning an integrative perspective when they lack clinical experience and developmentally feel anxious about their clinical competence. They feel the added pressure that may impact on their confidence and self-efficacy if they believe they will not do it well. Thus, it is important to validate their worries, present the advantages of IST, and ask them to treat learning IST as an experiment without fully committing to it.

THE SUPERVISOR: I understand your concern, Veronica. Some students expressed the same worry when they do not know much about integration. It does feel overwhelming to think you are going to integrate models when you know little about them. Integration does not begin after you have mastered all the therapy approaches. Applying an integrative systemic approach with careful attention to therapeutic alliance is a good start to produce effective treatment outcomes. There is no best way to train an integrative systemic therapist. However, when therapists learn an integrative approach first, the integrative method is like a bookshelf that stores and organizes all the clinical knowledge and interventions in a different order and location based on a theoretical foundation and a series of principles. Therapists can locate all the therapy models and research they learn later on this bookshelf. Then everything more easily fits together in the house, and therapists know when to use what. Integration provides metatheory of therapy theories and research. The reason I want to train integrative systemic therapists is I believe therapists, even at their early stage of learning, can learn a meta-approach that can benefit their long-term career development.

VERONICA: Oh, that's interesting. I see the value of learning an integrative approach. I was struggling to understand how different models could work together within a case. They seem not compatible. Thanks for having confidence in us. I am willing to try.

THE SUPERVISOR: Excellent. You don't have to be fully committed to it now. I will guide you throughout the process. How about I give you some articles to read and then we will have a mini-teaching meeting about IST?

VERONICA: Yes, I would be interested in reading them.

THE SUPERVISOR: Great. Briefly speaking, IST is a meta-perspective that provides guidelines and principles to integrative concepts and techniques from various therapy models as well as research. I will send you some references including two books and a few journal articles. Although they are quite long, in the first several weeks I want you to focus on two important tools: the IST essence diagram and the blueprint. These two figures, coupled with common factor research, guide clinical decisions in therapy, and are used a lot in supervision. After you familiarize yourself with these tools, I will introduce the theoretical pillars and hypothesizing and planning metaframeworks through additional readings. These metaframeworks guide your decisions about which concepts best explain a case, and which interventions and techniques are appropriate to use in specific clinical situations.

VERONICA: Sounds good.

THE SUPERVISOR: Okay, we have already talked about my goal for training an integrative systemic therapist via supervision. What are some of your goals?

VERONICA: I want to build confidence as a systemic therapist. I have seen a few clients. I found myself easily getting nervous in session and did not know what to do. I do not want clients to think I am not competent.

THE SUPERVISOR: Yes, let's list it in our supervision contract. As you know, it is very normal for new therapists in training to have self-doubts. We will work together to build your confidence. I consider it as a goal of developing your clinical competence because it may be manifested in all your therapy work.

VERONICA: That makes sense.

THE SUPERVISOR: What else?

VERONICA: What about any personal issues that are related to clinical competence? Can we talk about my own development in supervision?

THE SUPERVISOR: Did you mean "self of the therapist" topics? Absolutely. I always encourage my therapists to constantly reflect on how they can use themselves effectively in therapy and welcome them to bring it up in supervision. For example, I may ask for information about your family of origin or other past experiences if I think it is related to your clinical work. However, I want to make a clear distinction between the self-of-the-therapist topics and personal therapy because the boundary can get blurred if we do not pay attention to it. As your supervisor, although I may ask something about your personal life, it must be related to your goal of developing clinical competency instead of purely helping you to resolve any issues in your life. In other words, supervisors and therapists have distinct roles. I am only your supervisor. If there are personal struggles I observe which may interfere with your ability to see clients, I may recommend that you seek your own therapy.

VERONICA: Understood. Thanks for explaining it.

Self-of-the-therapist work is considered an important aspect of IST training and supervision. As in the vignette, the supervisor mentioned that she will ask Veronica about her family of origin and personal experiences in supervision. She also drew the boundary between supervision and therapy. She said that she would only ask if it were related to the therapist's clinical work or specific cases. The Person-of-the-Therapist Training (POTT, Aponte et al., 2009; Aponte, 2022) is incorporated in IST supervision and training. Please find more explanations in Chapter 6: Development of the Integrative Systemic Therapist.

In the first meeting, the supervisor and Veronica mutually agreed with the above goals (including following the profession's ethics guidelines) as well as the frequency and time of their meeting. Through collaborative discussions, they built a working alliance in the supervisory relationship and signed a supervision contract. To assist Veronica's understanding of IST, the supervisor assigned the two IST books (Pinsof et al., 2018; Russell et al., 2023) and some brief entries related to IST in *The Encyclopedia of Couple and Family Therapy* (e.g., Burgoyne, 2018; Breunlin, 2017; Taussig, 2019) for Veronica to read in the first two months, and later incorporated several mini-lectures in their supervision to briefly go over the IST theoretical underpinning known as the pillars, essence diagram, blueprint, hypothesizing and planning metaframeworks, and other guidelines such as the cost-effective guideline and the alliance priority guideline. Furthermore, to guide their supervision and train Veronica to conduct therapy using IST, the supervisor provided a supervision guide that lists the IST essence diagram and corresponding questions at each step of the essence for Veronica to reflect during and between supervision meetings. The supervision guide can be found in He et al. (2021). When they did case consultation, Veronica was asked to answer the supervisor's first question: "Where are you on the essence diagram?" before moving to the details of the case. Veronica absorbed the new knowledge quickly. After two months, upon Veronica's request, the supervisor provided more reading resources including the IST articles (e.g., Hardy et al., 2019; He et al., 2023; Russell & Breunlin, 2019). By having a Q & A portion, readings, and discussions in their supervision, after five months Veronica was able to conceptualize a clinical case using the IST essence diagram and blueprint. The supervisor conducted live supervision and provided first-hand guidance on the supervisor's cases. After nine months, Veronica was able to apply the IST approach in the therapy room and process it with the supervisor in supervision.

What Is IST Supervision?

We believe that the best supervision must be integrative, meaning it should incorporate multiple therapy models into an overall cohesive and theoretically sound supervision (Lee & Nelson, 2013; Lebow, 1997; Morgan &

Sprenkle, 2007). IST supervision is a meta-perspective of supervision, grounded in systemic theory and integration, which utilizes the IST's theoretical frameworks and practical guidelines in the process of supervision. It is not grounded in one specific strategy for intervention but incorporates many therapeutic strategies. As described in He et al. (2021), the goals of IST supervision are twofold. First, it provides supervisors with a theoretical framework to guide their therapists' clinical work and evaluate their progress and effectiveness in client care. Second, it helps supervisors to oversee and facilitate their therapists' overall development which refers to the acquisition of core competencies, including knowledge, skills, judgment, and use of self.

The Benefits of IST Supervision

IST supervision is an integrative metamodel that transcends the various theories contained in the models. IST posits that therapists can learn an integrative systemic approach as a foundation while simultaneously learning about other models, strategies, and interventions and drawing from them. When the therapist learns new concepts and interventions, it often is easy for them to integrate them into the IST framework. And IST provides a common ground for decision-making in therapy. Therefore, the IST supervisor would not encourage therapists to limit themselves to one particular model as their favorite to begin their learning and practice. And this works well with experienced clinicians who often continue learning new approaches and incorporating them into the IST framework; a task made easier by their not needing to abandon their existing expertise as they add new skills.

IST provides a theoretical framework that is compatible with all systemic therapies, but frees therapists from being limited to the core theory of a certain model. The literature on common factors suggests that a strong therapeutic alliance paired with a "good enough" level of competence is considered sufficient to produce desirable outcomes with many presenting issues (Sprenkle et al., 2009). As a result, IST assumes that therapists do not have to reach the most advanced stages of training in an approach to apply concepts and techniques from it; the level of skillfulness to apply an intervention can be assessed in the dialog between therapist and supervisor (Russell & Breunlin, 2019). For example, action methods or therapy approaches involving physical movement and expressive art techniques originate from multiple disciplines such as theatre, film, drama, and psychodrama. Yet the use of action method techniques would not require training within these disciplinary arts. That is to say that one would not need to be an expert in the method's origin to use this strategy. Exceptions are based on the supervisor's judgment that a particular intervention may require more intensive training, or a special clinical problem/population needs special treatment and extant knowledge. For example, implementing EMDR (eye movement desensitization and reprocessing) requires more specialized training than cognitive restructuring techniques (or reframing, from CBT).

In addition, from a multi-systemic perspective, IST integrates the modalities of psychotherapy, including individual, couple, and family therapy, and also bridges the mental health disciplines (i.e., psychology, social work, counseling, and marriage and family therapy) and their subfields such as clinical psychology, counseling psychology, school psychology, all of which have specialized foci. For example, psychology concentrates on an individual's thoughts, behaviors, emotions, and physiology/neurology. Marriage and family therapy (also called couple and family therapy) focuses on family dynamics and relationships. Social work promotes the interactions between individual development and social, economic, and cultural institutions as well as social change. Using the hypothesizing metaframeworks, which include factors at individual (biology, mind, self), family (organization, development, sequences, intergenerational patterns), and societal (gender, spirituality, culture) levels, IST considers all the primary domains of those mental health disciplines.

Furthermore, IST integrates individual-oriented models as well as systemic therapy models. For instance, a diverse array of methods such as chain analysis from dialectical behavior therapy (DBT), the "empty chair" technique from gestalt therapy (Perls et al., 1951), the psychological flexibility process of "cognitive defusion" from acceptance commitment therapy (ACT, Hayes et al., 2011) may be regarded as relevant when implementing a solution sequence that is linked to individuals' behaviors, thoughts, and emotions.

Finally, therapists are encouraged to be lifelong learners within the IST framework. According to the literature on psychotherapy, there is an overwhelming body of knowledge on clinical models, evidence-based therapies, new explanations about psychological and relational problems, common factors, therapeutic principles, and techniques (Russell & Breunlin, 2019). Regardless of the therapist's developmental stage, IST supervision serves as a template to integrate not only the existing therapy and supervision theories but also new empirical evidence, knowledge, therapy approaches, and techniques. It provides a complex conceptualization of clients' problems and solutions, so it can address a wider range of human behavior and problems.

Can Entry-level Therapists Practice IST?

Although most supervisors and educators would agree that becoming an integrative therapist is a long-term goal, one common question they raise is whether entry-level students in training can learn and practice an integrative approach. A metaphor that they would give is that students must learn how to walk before they can run. Therefore, their goal is to help students develop an in-depth understanding of one specific therapy model and the ability to apply it in clinical work. They may strongly discourage therapists from learning an integrative approach because they worry that students would be too overwhelmed to comprehend such an approach and thus lose confidence. Supervisors are also concerned that therapists will end up not doing well with their knowledge and skill in any methods of intervention if they invest in learning from an integrative perspective from the beginning.

At the first look, such concerns are reasonable. Upon closer examination, however, there are multiple issues with this train of thought. First, the idea that therapists will be overwhelmed in considering multiple frames for human problems is exaggerated. Further, an integrative approach that provides a clear plan for assessment and action is not more stressful to learn than a more narrowly focused approach. Therapists learn to work with intervention strategies in stages, and one important skill of the supervisor lies in helping the therapist expand their therapy repertoire in a way that maximizes their learning and effectiveness. Every therapy model has its assumptions, concepts, and series of interventions and techniques. Some therapeutic strategies require extensive training and supervision for therapists to develop their expertise. Any unfamiliar therapy approach will take time for both the supervisor and the therapist to learn. Further, many IST skills transcend models such as alliance-building and problem-solving. These tasks and how to do them are discussed in detail in the first book of this series (Russell et al., 2023).

Second, logically it makes sense to help therapists build expertise in working in the context of a more limited range of theoretical constructs and intervention, and hopefully they can expand their knowledge and skills to others later. That is the developmental trajectory of most therapists. Some therapists may synthesize two approaches sharing similar theoretical assumptions and use them together in clinical practice, which is considered eclecticism. However, they may not have an opportunity to learn how to integrate different models with the proper guidance from experienced supervisors.

On a related note, supervisors' readiness to adopt IST as their model of practice and supervision varies. As a result, supervisors need to reflect on their values, goals, and openness to determine if learning IST and IST supervision is a worthwhile investment. They also need to consider the external requirements of their academic programs, clinical sites, governing associations, culture, and broader society interests when making the decision. More discussion about the supervisor's development and the therapist's development can be found in Chapter 5 and 6 respectively.

Unique Characteristics of IST Supervision

IST supervision is consistent with many existing supervision models in a way that cultivates clinical competency in conducting systemic therapy and strengthens therapists' growth. Just like other systemic supervision models, the IST supervisor provides guidance for therapists to adhere to the ethical guidelines in their professions and local laws, develop capacities to effectively deliver treatment to address various populations and presenting issues, and conceptualize and intervene from a systemic lens. That said, the goals of IST supervision are the same as the majority of systemic supervision approaches. The differences exist in how to achieve those goals.

There are some unique methods in IST supervision. IST supervision fosters the therapist's ability to integrate the knowledge, concepts, and interventions from various therapy models and research based on the IST framework. On the other hand, supervision based on a singular therapy model, such as Bowenian family therapy, focuses on Bowenian concepts and interventions such as improving the therapist's skills in constructing a genogram, facilitating the family member's self-differentiation, and reducing anxiety. Thus, the way to evaluate clinical competency in Bowenian therapy is to evaluate the therapist's implementation of the basic knowledge and interventions from Bowenian family therapy theory as well as the therapy outcomes. IST supervision does not primarily focus on mastering a specific technique from a particular therapy model. Instead, IST supervision helps the therapist to use the IST tools including essence, blueprint, the hypothesizing and planning metaframeworks, and a few other guidelines in their clinical work effectively. When conducting case consultations or watching a live therapy session, the IST supervisor constantly checks if the therapist understands the problem sequence, solution sequence, and any potential constraints in the client system. The supervisor also helps the therapist to hypothesize, plan, and evaluate how to use knowledge and interventions from existing theories to implement a solution sequence or remove a constraint.

IST is a problem-centered approach. In supervision, there will be many occasions when the therapist brings questions and concerns on their own or the supervisor raises concerns about certain aspects of the therapist's clinical competence and development or their clients' well-being. It is typical that the supervisor would ask the therapist to discuss areas that get them stuck in therapy for case consultation purposes. It is an important moment for the supervisor to explore what the constraint is that keeps the therapist stuck. If the supervisor notices any mistakes that the therapist makes, they will provide such feedback in a non-critical way. Whenever those situations happen, the supervisor and the therapist should have open discussions and find ways to address the concerns or constraints. When solution sequences are successfully implemented and the constraints are removed, the therapist naturally gains competence. However, supervision is different from therapy due to different goals, roles, and relationships in therapy and supervision (Morgan & Sprenkle, 2007)—yet given the common-place practice of extrapolating therapy models into supervision, there are concerns about therapists being "therapized" using those models (Watkins et al., 2015). The application of IST in supervision could also run this risk. Therefore, one major modification from IST to IST supervision is to transform a problem-centered focus in IST to a growth-oriented approach in IST supervision. A growth-oriented approach specifically refers to a goal of promoting the therapist's clinical competency and development in IST.

In the following subsections, a few of the key characteristics of IST supervision will be explained, including its multi-systemic nature, focus on integration, the role of supervisors as well as the expectations for therapists. As shown in the supervision vignette at the beginning of the chapter, it is highly recommended that the supervisor and the therapist discuss and write a contract before they begin working together, including the specific goals, tasks, roles, and expectations for supervision. They can review their progress after a certain period and revise the goals if needed. It enables both parties to receive feedback and adjust based on the needs and development of the therapist with the consideration of any changes in the context of an academic program, an internship site, postgraduate training, or independent practice.

The Systemic Dimension of Supervision

Aligned with IST's ontological pillar, IST supervision is grounded in a twenty-first-century version of systems theory. Human systems consist of a nested hierarchy of subsystems that include society, community, family, relationship, and individual biology and psychology. Applying the ontological pillar to the context of supervision, IST supervision happens in an embedded hierarchy of subsystems that include society, community, graduate programs/internship agencies, supervisors, therapists, and clients. IST supervisors view therapists' development of competency within the context of the therapists' training background, the policy of their educational programs and agencies, the resources and values of the community, and the culture of the society.

Telehealth began to draw people's attention before COVID-19 and has been applied broadly in society during and after COVID-19. Entering a new era, online supervision becomes a viable choice that overcomes logistical and geographic barriers, and it brings opportunities and challenges. The influence of technology on supervision will be further discussed in Chapter 4. The supervision system is further nested in culture, community, and societal systems. For instance, IST supervision would look different when it is conducted by a supervisor in another culture or country as many contextual factors including policy and ethical requirements may change. For example, the political environment in certain geographic areas impacts supervision. In the United States, there are different views towards a few issues (e.g., LGBTQ+ rights and abortion rights) between the "red states" (states that favor the Republican Party) and "blue states" (states that prefer the Democratic Party). When the political opinions and policies contribute to the problem sequence, constraints, or solution sequence, the supervisor needs to guide the therapist to carefully consider those factors.

For all the subsystems in supervision, there are hierarchies, boundaries, and alliances between and among them. There is an inevitable hierarchy between the supervisor and the therapist, and the therapist and the client. Supervisors are ethically responsible for the clients' well-being and the actions of therapists in therapy. As a gatekeeper, the supervisor evaluates the therapist's capacity to conduct therapy effectively and must request the therapist to pause seeing clients if their competency is determined to be significantly impaired. When the therapist is obtaining new skills in specialty areas, the supervisor needs to monitor whether the therapist has gained appropriate education, training, and supervised experience to practice that skill. When the supervisor and the therapist have discrepant views about a case, which they often do when the therapist is at an advanced stage, the supervisor's opinion outweighs the therapist's, particularly when there is a concern about an ethical violation. However, that does not prevent supervision from being collaborative. The supervisor must avoid misuse of their power in setting directions and providing evaluations for supervision. Moreover, the supervisor should follow the ethical guidelines of the mental health profession. If the supervisor works onsite within an academic program or a mental health agency, there is a hierarchy between the supervisor and the setting because the supervisor needs to follow the policy of the program.

There should be a clear and flexible boundary between the supervisor and the therapist. Although the supervisor plays multiple roles such as a gatekeeper, an administrator, and a teacher, the professional boundary between the supervisor system and the client system must be maintained, and the supervisor should not provide therapy for the therapist or play the role of a friend. Furthermore, the supervisor must do everything to avoid dual relationships (e.g., attending the same church as the therapist or being involved in a romantic relationship with the therapist) that could interfere with professional judgment. Furthermore, this boundary should be flexible so that the supervisor welcomes the therapist's feedback and offers space for the therapist to struggle and grow their clinical competence that fits their developmental needs.

To ensure a safe environment for therapists to explore professional identity and develop competency, the supervisor must maintain a good supervisory alliance with the therapist. This alliance is reflected in a bond between the supervisor and the therapist and the consensus on goals and tasks during supervision. The bond between the supervisor and the therapist has some overlap with the bond between the therapist and the client, involving mutual trust, transparency, and honesty. It was found that supervisors' interpersonal attractiveness and expertise were rated important by the therapist (Anderson et al., 2000). One of the major constraints preventing therapists from disclosing the difficulties they meet during therapy is their fear of being judged or criticized by the supervisor. The supervisor needs to facilitate open communication and encouragement for the therapist to feel comfortable asking questions, sharing their different opinions with the supervisor, opening up about their self-of-the-therapist issues, and exploring their growing edges. The supervisor should also respect the therapist's confidentiality unless their behaviors contradict ethical codes or program policy. IST supervisors have their goals defined in IST supervision. Meanwhile, therapists may have more specific goals, such as increasing their confidence working with clients. It is important for IST supervisors to ask therapists about their goals so that they can reach an agreement. It is equally essential for IST supervisors to discuss the specific tasks involved in achieving the goals.

In IST, the alliance priority guideline states that the therapist would prioritize alliance when making a clinical decision unless doing so interferes with the treatment effectiveness or integrity. It is appropriate for the therapist to provide direct feedback to clients as the therapist determines it is clinically necessary, even though the client does not want to hear it. However, the therapist can never force the client to do anything if the client objects because it risks the client's autonomy. In IST supervision, the supervisor would still prioritize alliance with the therapist to provide a nurturing learning environment unless doing so violates ethical guidelines or poses threats to clients' well-being. Because the hierarchy exists between the supervisor and the therapist as well as the gatekeeper role the supervisor plays, the supervisor can request the therapist to do something or cease doing something even though the therapist disagrees. For instance, if the supervisor decides the risk of working with the client outweighs the benefits, whereas the therapist insists on seeing the client, the supervisor can request the therapist to stop working with the client.

The Integrative Dimension of Supervision

In the literature on integration in psychotherapy, concepts such as theoretical integration, technical eclectic, common factors, and assimilative integration have been widely discussed (Castonguay et al., 2015). IST is a combination of theoretical integration and common factors. It has a comprehensive theoretical framework that helps therapists to work across various therapy models (not just two or three), and it incorporates common factors of therapy. The IST essence presents the process of conducting therapy, the blueprint guides the moment-to-moment clinical decision-making, and the hypothesizing and planning metaframeworks determine what concepts and interventions to use at any given time of therapy. Together with other guidelines, they can be used in supervision to facilitate therapists' theoretical integration.

In addition to integrating various therapy theories, IST supervision incorporates common factors of therapy and supervision. Common factors refer to a set of underlying common variables in therapy that may account for the majority of outcome change regardless of therapy models. There have been efforts to supervise therapists mainly based on common factors (D'Aniello & Fife, 2017; Karam et al., 2015). There is also literature identifying common factors that MFT supervisors can follow to facilitate effective supervision, including providing support and compliments, supportive collaboration, and the ability to play multiple supervisory roles (Morgan & Sprenkle, 2007; Watkins et al., 2015). As IST has already involved common factors to guide therapy, those common factors for therapy and supervision also apply to IST supervision.

Supervisor's Roles and Responsibilities

The main roles IST supervisors play are mentor, teacher, coach, and administrator (including a gatekeeping role) (see Morgan & Sprenkle, 2007). The IST supervisor assumes a leadership role and communicates with therapists in a warm yet direct way. The IST supervisor encourages and compliments therapists' improvement and progress. IST supervisors do not hesitate to share their thoughts about therapists' cases and development if they think therapists are ready to hear them. To maintain a good supervisory alliance, IST supervisors gauge what would be an appropriate way and the right timing to provide constructive feedback.

IST supervisors may decide how much to share their opinions about a case with the therapist depending on the therapist's developmental needs. When the therapist is at the early stage of seeing clients, the supervisor may provide more specific directions about what and how to intervene. When the therapist is at an advanced level with more clinical experience, the supervisor expects therapists to be more independent and, therefore, challenges the therapist to generate their own hypothesis and plan.

In addition to promoting the therapist's competency, the IST supervisor assumes the responsibility of gatekeeper and constantly evaluates the therapist's competency, use of ethics, and professionalism. If a therapist does not meet the ethical standard of their profession, the supervisor needs to generate a plan for the therapist to improve. This usually requires collaboration with the setting where the supervision and/or clinical agency takes place. If the supervisor determines the therapist is no longer competent to deliver treatment, the supervisor should consult with a supervisor mentor, academic department, or consultant and then advise the therapist to either take a break, refer the client to another therapist, or terminate the therapist's enrollment in the program.

Expectations for Therapists

There are similarities with the expectations for therapists in IST supervision compared to other supervision models, such as being professional, honest, and ethical. The therapist is expected to interact with the supervisor and other therapists (if in group supervision) in a respectful and professional manner. More importantly, the therapist should seek help from the supervisor whenever they are uncertain about clinical decision-making. The therapist should stay open to feedback from the supervisor and other group members. In circumstances where the therapist disagrees with the supervisor or other group members, the therapist can express their thoughts, while trying to understand others' perspectives. Because it is sometimes easy to criticize oneself and others when the therapist feels nervous, the therapist needs to hold a compassionate and supportive stance with themselves, clients, and other therapists (in group supervision).

The unique expectation for IST therapists is to have at least a certain amount of commitment to practice an integrative, systemic therapy approach and establish the identity of an IST therapist. As demonstrated in the supervision vignette, just like Veronica, IST is new to many therapists. In this case, the supervisor needs to introduce IST to them and set up an open discussion about whether learning IST would be of interest to the therapist. In most cases, therapists are open to practicing more than one therapy model and it is not difficult for them to attempt learning about IST in supervision. IST is usually not a good fit for therapists who are either not committed to practicing systemic therapy or not interested in learning more than one therapy model. When this happens, the supervisor needs to inform the therapist about the mismatch and most likely suggest they find another supervisor. Ultimately, both the supervisor and the therapist need to reach an agreement about the goals and tasks of their supervision to make supervision effective.

The Setting of IST Supervision

Supervision usually occurs in an academic setting, at external sites to fulfill the academic requirement, or at postgraduate agency settings. It depends on the requirements of the academic program and the mental health profession, but sometimes therapists can work at their own or others' private practice settings. In this case, they receive supervision from the private practice owner or hire a supervisor outside of the private practice setting.

Supervision in Academic Programs

In an academic setting, there are two types of supervision provided: supervision provided to therapists who conduct therapy at their external internship site and supervision offered to therapists who do therapy at the onsite clinic of the academic institution. It is possible that a therapist may have two supervisors, one in the academic program and one at the external site. In certain academic programs, the therapist may have more than one supervisor—for example, one group supervisor and one individual supervisor. It is important for an IST supervisor to work together with other supervisors as they are all in the indirect system of the therapist system. It requires extra effort for the supervisor to contact other supervisors who supervise the same therapist. Supervisors in the same academic program have the advantage of working collaboratively because of proximal location, shared curriculum, and supervision expectations.

The mission of the academic programs, as well as their administration, directly impacts supervision when supervision is embedded within academic programs. To let the administrators and faculty of the program buy into the idea of integrative systemic training is essential to build a supportive environment for therapists' development in IST. The academic program may have different levels of acceptance and support for integrative training. Providing supervision in a program that values integrative, systemic training is easier compared to a program that heavily values singular model training. When the program's curriculum involves teaching IST, the supervisor would receive strong support for implementing IST supervision. In contrast, if the program does not support supervision to be integrative, it will be a significant constraint for conducting IST supervision. We suspect that most programs are in the middle: they do not teach IST while they are not against IST. In this case, the supervisor has some flexibility to decide how they would like to conduct supervision.

Supervision in Postgraduate Agencies or Private Practice

Supervision in postgraduate agencies is more straightforward because therapists do not have to consider the requirements of an academic program and they have more flexibility to find an agency that fits their needs and clinical interests. Developmentally, therapists have more clinical experiences and knowledge to determine what clinical settings and populations are the best for developing their expertise before they get fully licensed. For instance, some therapists want to grow their skills in working with couples and thus they choose to work at a couple therapy clinic. Some therapists are interested in working at community mental health clinics or medical centers. If the therapist receives supervision from an onsite supervisor, the types of agencies largely determine the possible training, including supervision, they will receive. For instance, the training and supervision received by therapists working a couple therapy clinic may primarily focus on couple therapy. For therapists working in medical settings, their training may be about the collaboration with medical staff to provide integrated health care.

Therapists may have supervisors onsite or supervisors offsite. If the therapist can find a supervisor offsite, they have greater freedom to select a supervisor who matches their interests. Regardless of supervision onsite or not, supervisors may be more flexible to choose their supervision approach. However, if the supervisor adopts the IST supervision method, they need to find ways to provide IST supervision to fit the client populations and typical problems. For example, how can IST supervision be adapted to sex therapy? This may require the supervisor to have extra training and clinical experiences in sex therapy and understand the typical problem sequences and solution sequences pertaining to people's sexual problems. Certain hypothesizing metaframeworks are more relevant to some presenting problems. In this case, biology, development, gender, and culture metaframeworks may be more related to the problem and solution sequences in sex therapy.

Some licensed/experienced therapists in agencies or private practices are interested in advancing their skills and expertise in systemic integration. Although they do not need supervision for independent practice, they would seek out supervision from an IST supervisor. The therapist most likely has a basic level of clinical competence in their field through their prior training and experience. They may acknowledge the importance of integration training. They perhaps have learned about integration and even IST through readings, conferences, and workshops which prompts them to seek IST supervision. Therefore, the supervisor perhaps does not need to demonstrate the rationale of the IST supervision such as how it was done in the vignette with Veronica. The supervisor is recommended to ask about the therapist's existing expertise and discuss their expectations and specific goals. Making a connection between the therapist's existing skills and IST is important to help them transition to an integrative systemic way of conceptualizing and intervening while still keeping their specialty. The goals of the supervision stay the same: improving clinical competence in general and promoting development. However, the emphasis is likely to be placed on clinical competence in utilizing IST and the therapist's long-term career development on systemic integration. Similar to the postgraduate setting, the supervisor helps the therapist to adapt IST to the clientele and presenting issues they work with, which may involve heavily focusing on some hypothesizing and planning metaframeworks.

Conclusion

Chapter 2 summarizes the goals, benefits, unique characteristics, and setting of IST supervision. Our hope is that supervisors and therapists can use this overview as a starting point for setting up the structure and organization of their supervision and forming a supervisory relationship, which requires certain flexibility and negotiations so they can adapt it to their settings and cultural context. We encourage the supervisor and the therapist to have a candid conversation about whether those goals and expectations fit their interests and needs.

References

Anderson, S. A., Schlossberg, M., & Rigazio-DiGilio, S. (2000). Family therapy supervisees' evaluations of their best and worst supervision experiences. *Journal of Marital and Family Therapy*, 26(1), 79–91. https://doi.org/10.1111/j.1752-0606.2000.tb00278.x.

Aponte, H. J. (2022). The soul of therapy: The therapist's use of self in the therapeutic relationship. *Contemporary Family Therapy*, 44(2), 136–143.

Aponte, H. J., Powell, F. D., Brooks, S., Watson, M. F., Litzke, C., Lawless, J., & Johnson, E. (2009). Training the person of the therapist in an academic setting. *Journal of Marital and Family Therapy*, 35(4), 381–394.

Burgoyne, N. (2018). Blueprint for therapy in metaframeworks: Transcending the models of family therapy. In Lebow, J., Chambers, A., & Breunlin, D. (Eds.), *The encyclopedia of couple and family therapy*. Springer. https://doi.org/10.1007/978-3-319-15877-8_912-1.

Breunlin, D. C. (2017). Theory of constraints in couple and family therapy. In Lebow, J., Chambers, A., & Breunlin, D. (Eds.), *The encyclopedia of couple and family therapy*. Springer. https://doi.org/10.1007/978-3-319-15877-8_913-1.

Castonguay, L. G., Eubanks, C. F., Goldfried, M. R., Muran, J. C., & Lutz, W. (2015). Research on psychotherapy integration: Building on the past, looking to the future. *Psychotherapy Research*, 25(3), 365–382. https://doi.org/10.1080/10503307.2015.1014010.

D'Aniello, C., & Fife, S. T. (2017). Common factors' role in accredited MFT training programs. *Journal of Marital and Family Therapy*, 43(4), 591–604. https://doi.org/10.1111/jmft.12218.

Hardy, N. R., Brosi, M. W., & Gallus, K. L. (2019). Integrative systemic therapy: Lessons on collaboration and training for the 21st century. *Journal of Marital and Family Therapy*, 45(2), 206–218. https://doi.org/10.1111/jmft.12332.

Hayes, S. C., Strosahl, K. D., & Wilson, K. G. (2011). *Acceptance and commitment therapy: The process and practice of mindful change*. Guilford Press.

He, Y., Hardy, N., & Russell, W. (2021). Integrative systemic supervision: Promoting therapists' theoretical integration in systemic therapy. *Family Process*, 61(1), 58–75. https://doi.org/10.1111/famp.12667.

He, Y., Hardy, N., Fisher, A., & Lokatama, I. (2023). The development of the Integrative Systemic Therapist. *Fokus på familien*, 51(4), 315–331. https://doi.org/10.18261/fokus.51.4.4.

Karam, E. A., Blow, A. J., Sprenkle, D. H., & Davis, S. D. (2015). Strengthening the systemic ties that bind: Integrating common factors into marriage and family therapy curricula. *Journal of Marital and Family Therapy*, 41(2), 136–149. https://doi.org/10.1111/jmft.12096.

Lee, R. E., & Nelson, T. S. (2013). *The contemporary relational supervisor*. Routledge.

Lebow, J. (1997). The integrative revolution in couple and family therapy. *Family Process*, 36(1), 1–17. https://doi.org/10.1111/j.1545-5300.1997.00001.x.

Morgan, M. M., & Sprenkle, D. H. (2007). Toward a common-factors approach to supervision. *Journal of Marital and Family Therapy*, 33(1), 1–17. https://doi.org/10.1111/j.1752-0606.2007.00001.x.

Perls, F., Hefferline, G., & Goodman, P. (1951). *Gestalt therapy*. Julian Press.

Pinsof, W. M., Breunlin, D. C., Russell, W. P., Lebow, J. L., Rampage, C., & Chambers, A. L. (2018). *Integrative systemic therapy: Metaframeworks for problem solving with individuals, couples, and families*. American Psychological Association.

Russell, W. P., Breunlin, D. C., & Sahebi, B. (2023). *Integrative systemic therapy in practice: A clinician's handbook*. Routledge.

Russell, W. P., & Breunlin, D. C. (2019). Transcending therapy models and managing complexity: Suggestions from integrative systemic therapy. *Family Process*, 58(3), 641–655. https://doi.org/10.1111/famp.12482.

Sprenkle, D., Davis, S., & Lebow, J. (2009). *Common factors in couple and family therapy: The overlooked foundation for effective practice.* Guilford Press.

Taussig, D. (2019). Sequences in couple and family therapy. In Lebow, J., Chambers, A., & Breunlin, D. (Eds.), *The encyclopedia of couple and family therapy* (pp. 2624–2629). Springer. https://doi.org/10.1007/978-3-319-49425-8_915.

Watkins, M. (2015). Psychosocial accompaniment. *Journal of Social and Political Psychology,* 3(1), 324–341. https://doi.org/10.5964/jspp.v3i1.103.

Chapter 3

Supervising Cases with the IST Perspective

This chapter will demonstrate how to use IST's essence diagram, blueprint, matrix, and guidelines (described in Chapter 1) to conduct IST supervision. Specifically, this chapter uses supervision vignettes to illustrate the steps of the IST's essence diagram, including convening a direct client system and defining the problem, locating a problem in a problem sequence, identifying and implementing a solution sequence, evaluating outcomes, identifying the constraints, attempting to lift the constraints, evaluating outcomes again, implementing and maintaining the solution sequence, and finally termination. The blueprint and other tools of IST are discussed in the context of the essence steps.

It is important for therapists to understand that IST's problem-solving steps are recursive. Clients may present more than one problem or, as a problem is being addressed, they may identify an additional concern. When this is the case, the therapist asks them to prioritize and order their therapy goals, as it is confusing to work on several goals at the same time unless they are closely related and share a lot of overlap in their problem sequence and solution sequence. The therapist may have the misconception that they would only go through the steps of the IST essence once with a case, but clients often have more than one problem to solve. Thus, once each problem is solved, or sufficiently improved, the therapist will move onto the next goal on the client's list and utilize the essence diagram all over again for any subsequent goals until all the goals have been addressed.

Step 1: Convene a Direct Client System and Define the Problem

The first step in the IST essence diagram is to determine a direct client system and define the problem. These two tasks are simultaneous co-occurring processes.

Convene a Direct Client System

In IST, the concept of the client system adds more nuances to decide whom to invite for therapy. The direct client system includes the group of people

DOI: 10.4324/9781003146841-3

who play a key role in the maintenance and resolution of the problem. It is recommended that the therapist begins the work with a relational client system (i.e., family or couple) before moving to individual sessions. When couples present a couple problem, IST typically begins with the couple and not the family. The exceptions occur when the therapist thinks it is appropriate to begin with an individual client or when the client has a strong preference for who should attend therapy.

The term "family" here has a broader definition than just the nuclear family members. It can include parents/caregivers, children, siblings, intergenerational members such as grandparents and extended relations, friends, teachers, and community members. For reasons illustrated by Breunlin and Jacobsen (2014), many therapists including those with a family therapy training background do not typically see the whole family in their clinical practice. Therapists may primarily work with subsystems of the family or an individual family member. For example, some therapists may see children for individual sessions without regularly meeting with their parents or siblings. Although there may be benefits in doing that, seeing the whole family provides the therapist with a more complete view of the system through direct observation. It also offers the therapist an opportunity to directly intervene with the system as the presenting problem often occurs in or is influenced by that relational context.

Therapists encounter familiar challenges when convening a direct client system. Regardless of their stage of development as therapists, some have primarily worked with individual clients, and they may perceive working with families as uncomfortable or unnecessary. Most individual therapy approaches and a few systemic therapy models state that changing an individual person's thoughts, behaviors, and/or feelings is sufficient to resolve the problem or change the family system. To help therapists prioritize working with the relational system, the supervisor may need to provide a strong rationale to begin therapy with a whole family system. For example, the supervisor may assign readings about family systems theory, articulate the advantages of multiple family members attending therapy, or discuss with the therapist the potential roadblocks for doing so. For example, the first author assigns a peer-reviewed journal article written by Breunlin and Jacobsen (2014) and asks her therapists to discuss the benefits of inviting family members to the therapy. Based on the article and their knowledge of systems theory, her therapists often acknowledge the advantages of working with the whole family. The first author then invites her therapists to brainstorm strategies for involving the family members and asks the therapists to enact the strategies in role-plays.

Therapists may lack experience in working with families. Therapists may doubt their competence: Am I able to handle conflicts that may occur? How do I help clients understand that there are multiple truths? How can I validate each of their perspectives? What should I do if one member is blamed for their problem? Would it be overwhelming for me to track the problem sequences among so many people? The supervisor normalizes therapists' discomfort and provides detailed guidance (including role-plays) to enhance their skills with conducting family sessions and increase their confidence. For example, the first author showed a video of an initial phone call with a client therapist in which the therapist invited the family to therapy. The therapist in this video presented a strong rationale and responds to the caller's hesitation to involve other family members. Then therapists in supervision were asked to utilize or adapt what the therapist says in several role-plays when the pretended clients showed various levels of resistance. This kind of exercise will be more effective in group supervision when the members can alternate playing the clients and the therapist and support each other's learning.

The supervisor ensures that the therapist understands that there are occasions when meeting with the whole family is not practical or desirable. There can be logistical issues such as scheduling conflicts, transportation barriers, a lack of childcare resources, and distances. Sometimes family members are unwilling to meet with the therapist due to mental health stigma, perceptions that they are irrelevant to the problem or treatment, or avoidance of taking responsibility for the problem. Culture plays a key role in families' intention to attend therapy. For instance, in individualistic cultures, individuals take pride in being independent and therefore may not want to involve others in their therapy. In collectivist cultures, maintaining harmonious relationships with others is essential. However, due to mental health stigma and poor mental health literacy, people in collectivist cultures are often reluctant to seek professional help for individual or relational problems. When family members are strongly against attending therapy, the therapist should prioritize the therapeutic alliance and respect their opinions. It may be worthwhile to bring the suggestion of involving other key family members up again after building a strong therapeutic alliance with the client system.

There are also situations in which inviting the whole family to the first session is inappropriate (e.g., couples who specifically request couple therapy) or potentially harmful (e.g., domestic violence, abuse). The supervisor coaches the therapist to carefully consider the potential benefits and risks associated with decisions about whom to convene for a first session and subsequent sessions. The supervisor reminds the therapist that there may be other opportunities to invite additional members of the system as the therapy progresses.

Because the concept of the client system is new to therapists, their supervisors should not assume that the therapist knows how to determine which members of the client system should attend sessions. The decision is a collaborative one that involves developing a hypothesis about whom to convene, communicating this to the client, providing a justification for the need to involve others in therapy, and stepping back if the client is strongly against the suggestion. The supervisor encourages the therapist to keep several questions in mind: Should I accept the preference of the person who initiates therapy? How can I explain my suggestion for who should attend therapy? If the initiating person rejects my suggestion, how far should I push it? Will it hurt our therapeutic alliance if the client does not like my suggestion? Answering these questions must always include consideration of IST's Alliance Priority Guideline (Pinsof et al., 2018; Russell et al., 2023). The following vignette demonstrates how the supervisor works with this scenario.

Mike, a cisgender White male student in a master's degree in Marriage and Family Therapy program located in the United States. Mike, having just begun his clinical internship, consulted on a case with his supervisor, Emily. Emily was a cisgender White female who had her own private practice while serving as adjunct faculty in a Marriage and Family Therapy program. She had received training to practice IST and was an IST supervisor. She also provided IST supervision to therapists in private practice. Mike received a request from the clinic director to conduct individual therapy with a male client at the program's onsite clinic. Mike has not had direct contact with the client yet; however, he learned from the clinic director that the client's wife called first on her husband's behalf and the male client followed up. When asked about the therapy goal, the male client mentioned to the clinic coordinator that he would like to improve his coping strategies during the COVID-19 pandemic, enhance communication skills, as well as address grief as he recently lost a good friend. Without any direct interactions with the client, Mike sought advice from Emily about whom to invite to therapy.

MIKE: I am a little confused. The wife called first and then the husband called and said he wanted individual therapy. Should I just see him alone or invite his wife to come for the first session?

EMILY: Good question. Are you sure that the wife called just to get treatment for her husband?

MIKE: Yes, that's what I heard from Natalie, our clinical coordinator. She directly talked to each of them. However, because the male client mentioned communication skills, I thought there might be some benefits of inviting his wife to come.

EMILY: Understood. You are figuring out the first step of the IST essence diagram—convening a direct client system and defining the problem. You are trying to decide whom to invite for therapy based on the information you have.

MIKE: Exactly. I want to consult with you because IST's interpersonal guideline states that we should prioritize working with a relational system rather than individuals. As you know, I want to work with a family system instead of just an individual client. But I am not sure whether it applies here as the male client requested individual therapy.

EMILY: I am glad that you are being thoughtful about who will be in the direct client system at the beginning of therapy as it is an important first step. I also appreciate that you are thinking about the relational system in your decision-making. It seems you do not have sufficient information to determine whom to invite. Is that right? How about collecting more information from him? There are two ways. The first way is to reach out to the male client directly by phone and ask him to clarify what might be the primary reasons for him to come to therapy and explore the possibility of convening a relational system for therapy. The second approach is to gather more information from him during the first session to discuss who will attend subsequent sessions. What do you think?

MIKE: Yes, that's a good idea. Since we have already scheduled the first meeting, I will wait till the first session so I will have enough time to do an assessment. Is that okay?

Emily sensed Mike's reluctance to call the male client and gather more information on the phone. He understood that Mike might be nervous to reach out as he is still new to the therapy process. To ease Mike's anxiety, Emily decided to follow Mike's proposal.

EMILY: That works. If you and the male client decide that a dyadic or family context is more appropriate, you will want to balance your alliance with other family members as you have already met alone with him once.

MIKE: Sure.

EMILY: Let's discuss what might be some questions you want to ask him. What do you think?

MIKE: I would like to know what he meant by "communication skills." The other two goals are more individual-focused. If the communication issues between him and his wife are the main problem, I would suggest inviting his wife to come.

EMILY: That's a great start. I partially agree. Although the client mentioned coping strategies during COVID-19 and grief, you do not have enough information to clearly define the problem. Instead of taking what the client said at face value, you will want to learn more about the problem in your first meeting. Even when goals are individual-oriented, as a systemic therapist, you also want to put those issues in a problem sequence and figure out who is involved in the repetitive problematic cycle. It is likely that inviting others will be helpful for those goals as well. What else would you like to know?

MIKE: I guess I want to know if the male client wants to include others in his therapy. What if he is strongly against it?

EMILY: Great question. You can make a recommendation to the client based on your evaluation. Although IST encourages therapists to begin with a relational client system, you will not want to force him to invite anyone he does not want to invite. That's the alliance priority guideline. There are other things you need to consider. For example, what is his priority goal? Is each of his goals related to his partner or others in his family? Might anyone in his network contribute significantly to the problem sequence or the solution sequence? How beneficial would it be to invite them to attend therapy? Are they willing to join therapy regularly? Or would they be willing to attend a session or two to provide their perspectives or show support?

MIKE: Wow, that's a lot of things to consider. If I get it right, I need to first collect information and identify the problem. The next step is to determine who may be involved in the maintenance or resolution of the problem. I must discuss my thoughts with the client and reach an agreement.

EMILY: Exactly. Let me know how it goes, and we will talk more when we have more information.

In the above conversations between Mike and his supervisor, Emily, they primarily talked about who should be involved in the direct client system based on Mike's assessment of the problem sequences and client's feedback. Ideally, therapists talk to clients who seek therapy directly on the phone when they schedule their first session. In this circumstance, the therapist can quickly assess the problem and offer the client suggestions about who should be invited to therapy. Because Mike spoke to the client and he is a novice therapist, Emily did not ask him to contact him through a phone call before the first session.

It is not unusual for therapists (even experienced therapists) to struggle with the question of whom they will invite for therapy. Notably, the initial decision can be changed after collecting more information and feedback in the first session. The supervisor helps therapists learn to make systemically informed decisions based on the presenting problem, clients' needs, and the therapist's clinical judgment instead of assuming that the type of problem identified at intake dictates an assignment to individual, couple, or family therapy. Further, in IST the decisions about who will attend sessions (direct client system) may evolve as new hypotheses are developed and discussed.

Define the Problem

One of the most important tasks for therapists in the initial stage of therapy is to clearly define the problem and reach a consensus with clients about the problem. It often takes at least one therapy session to define the problem, although the therapist may have a preliminary sense of it from the first phone call. The therapist should not define the problem purely based on the initiating client's report, though. Instead, the therapist needs to thoroughly explore the problem in the first session and, assuming more than one client attends the session, collect information from all those in attendance and observe the relational dynamics of the family. By gathering feedback from all members, the therapist can see if they share a similar definition of the problem. If the client system disagrees, the therapist revises the problem definition until they can reach an agreement. If there are multiple goals/problems, the clients also need to agree with the order in which they will be addressed. The clinical complexities related to defining the problem in IST are discussed in Russell et al. (2023).

The supervisor needs to be mindful of two common mistakes that therapists make early in their training. The first common mistake is that due to a lack of clinical experience and an eagerness to help the client system, therapists may take the clients' initial description of the problem at face value and jump to providing interventions without a more complete understanding of the problem. Lacking a thorough assessment of the problem poses a risk of forming an inaccurate hypothesis about the problem and problem sequence, and therefore constitutes an inadequate solution sequence. Inaccurate assessment of the problem delays treatment progress and can damage the therapeutic alliance. The second common mistake is that therapists may over-evaluate to the degree that they gather too much information unrelated to the presenting problem and, therefore, lose sight of what the clients seek to accomplish. They may then take this overload of information to supervision and thereby distract the supervisor from helping to clarify the therapist's hypothesis (formulation) about the problem. To avoid this situation, the supervisor should explicitly ask whether the therapist has a formulation of the problem, whether the therapist has shared a formulation with the client system, and whether the client system agrees with it. During case discussion and live supervision, the supervisor determines whether the therapist jumps too fast or is over-assessing and explores with them their reasons for doing so in a non-judgmental way. When the therapist is off track, the supervisor gently brings them back. The supervisor can ask such questions as "What information did you collect to define the problem?", "Have the clients clarified just what they mean by the terms they use to define the problem?", "Did members of the system agree or disagree on the definition of the problem(s)?" and "How do you know the client system agrees with your formulation of the problem?"

More experienced therapists can define the problem quickly. When learning IST, they are challenged to shift from conceptualizing the problem based on specific models to a more integrative way of looking at the problem. For example, a therapist who was trained as a structural family therapist during their graduate training now, after years of practice, wants to become an integrative therapist while still utilizing structural family therapy interventions. The therapist may readily conceptualize the problem as a function of family structure where parents do not exhibit a functional leadership role or the boundaries between family subsystems are unclear. In such a case, the supervisor can validate that it is helpful to see the case through structural family therapy theory, but then bring the therapist's attention back to the client system's concerns. The supervisor would say something like "It is great that you utilize the structural family therapy concepts to understand the problem. Now let's step back and try to know more about what is going on in the system related to the client's concerns."

Step 2: Locate a Problem in a Problem Sequence

After clearly defining the problem(s) and identifying a direct client system, the next step is to locate a presenting problem in a problem sequence. This step is essential because it transforms the conceptualization of the problem from its initial description to a simple systemic formulation of the process of how it unfolds and, typically, from an individual to a relational focus. Individual therapy approaches often view clients' presenting problems as primarily existing internally in an individual's mind. Therefore, the interventions of individual therapy approaches are designed to alter individuals' cognitions, behaviors, or emotions with the belief that changing those can resolve the problem. This approach is helpful at times; however, this type of conceptualization does not attend sufficiently to the fact that a problem is not isolated from its environment and context. IST supervisors help therapists see that when the conceptualization of the problem is narrowly defined at an individual level, it misses the opportunity to change the environment and interpersonal relationships which may be related to the problem. For example, a child's behavioral problem may exist in the context of parents' marital conflicts, sibling conflicts, or peer bullying at school. If the therapist does not think those things are related, they would not be able to intervene in these contexts, such as referring parents for couple therapy, seeing the siblings together for conflict resolution, or contacting school counselors and teachers for implementing anti-bullying interventions at the school. On the other hand, some systemic therapists pay exclusive attention to the interactions with others and the social context while ignoring the fact that the problem can have significant individually focused dimensions. Having the ability to track both the interpersonal and intrapsychic problem sequences is crucial. The supervisor helps the therapist to recognize the impact and potential constraints of their pre-existing beliefs and prior training on their treatment focus.

As is the case with the essence steps of defining the problem, some therapists tend to provide solutions or interventions for problem sequences that are not thoroughly understood. This can be a result of feeling eager and/or nervous to demonstrate one's competence to clients and the supervisor, and can lead to matching the name of the problem to interventions known to address that problem type. In recent decades, many evidence-based therapies have been developed, which are supported by empirical research as treatments for certain psychological problems. For example, cognitive behavioral therapy (Beck, 2011) has been shown to treat depression and anxiety disorders effectively (Butler et al., 2006). Attachment-based family therapy (Diamond et al., 2014) has been found to effectively treat adolescents' depression and suicidality (Diamond et al., 2016). While it is valuable to implement evidence-based treatments, they are often designed to address problems that occur in one of the subsystems of the family and do not account for the impact of other subsystems or the full family system on the presenting problems. The IST supervisor, therefore, needs to facilitate a more complete view of the problem sequences by expanding therapists' perceptions of different subsystems and contexts.

> To help identify the problem sequences, the supervisor can ask questions about the temporal relationships between events and interactions, the frequency, intensity and duration of the problem, and family members' behaviors, thoughts, and feelings during the sequential events related to the problem that occurs over time.
>
> (He et al., 2021)

To track the problem sequences, it is helpful to ask clients for specific examples of their interactions when the problem occurs. The supervisor can ask therapists, "Have you learned what happens before, during, and after the occurrence of the problem?", "What do each of the family members think, feel, and do during the sequential events around the problem?", "What interactions between family members have you observed in the sessions?" The supervisor may also ask the frequency, intensity, and duration of the problem and find out if the problem sequence occurs repetitively across situations. The supervisor may ask, "Have you checked if the problem sequence applies to other situations or contexts?" The following vignette is used to demonstrate how the supervisor helps the therapist track the problem sequence.

Vignette

Nina, a newly licensed White cisgender female psychologist, received supervision from her supervisor, Emily, who was an IST supervisor. Nina had some experience working with couples in her doctoral program. She became interested in IST and found Emily to supervise her. The supervision, including live supervision, was conducted remotely through HIPAA-compliant Zoom videoconferencing. In one of their supervision sessions, Nina introduced a case of a cisgender heterosexual White middle-class couple seeking therapy. The female partner (Charlotte) was 27 years old, working with children having special needs in an elementary school. The male partner (James) was 29 years old, and he was a mechanical engineer. They had been dating for a year and a half. The couple reported that they had a stable relationship without major conflicts. They sought therapy to understand each other better, identify triggers in their maladaptive interactions, and receive psychoeducation from the therapist about how to improve their relationship.

Nina had worked with the couple for six sessions before she sought a live supervision session with Emily. Emily asked Nina about her plan and goal for the live session. Nina mentioned that she was planning to understand the couple's problem sequence of a conflict that concerned them and begin identifying a solution sequence. This plan was consistent with one of the clients' goals—identify triggers for their conflict. Emily agreed and asked how Nina would focus on this goal during the session. Nina proposed to make the goal of the session clear at the start of the session and seek client agreement with it. Then, if the couple talks about other things that are irrelevant to this agenda, Nina will interrupt them and gently direct them back to their goal.

Emily joined Nina's telehealth session and stayed muted with her camera off throughout the session. Nina let her clients know in advance about Emily's presence and they completed appropriate paperwork for clients to consent to live supervision. Nina also let her clients know that there would be a ten-minute break halfway through the session during which they will be in the waiting room while she consults with Emily.

NINA: Good to see you today.

CHARLOTTE: Nice to see you too.

NINA: Today I want to continue our discussion from the last session. I know one of your goals is to identify triggers for conflict that occur in your interactions.

CHARLOTTE: Yes. I want to know more about my triggers so I can avoid having conflicts with James.

NINA: Great. My plan for today's session is to focus on figuring out what is really going on during your couple interaction and what can be potentially changed. Are you both okay with this plan?

JAMES: Sure.

CHARLOTTE: Yes.

NINA: Okay. We can start with some concrete examples. Can the two of you think of a recent conflict? Let's understand it more.

CHARLOTTE: I can think of an example easily. As you know, last Sunday was Valentine's Day. We planned to have a date night and go out for dinner. When we were about to leave home, I asked James which restaurant we would go to. He said that he reserved an Indian restaurant. I immediately got angry because he knows that I don't like Indian food.

NINA: So, Charlotte, you got angry. How did you respond, James?

JAMES: (paused for a moment): I did not know what to say. Then I just apologized.

CHARLOTTE: Yes, he did not respond quickly. When he apologized, I didn't even know if he understood what went wrong. It was so frustrating. I felt like he did not care about what I liked. I assumed that we were going to a restaurant that we both like.

NINA: (turned to both): Got it. If there is anything each of you can do differently to prevent this conflict from happening, what would you do?

CHARLOTTE: I think he needs to change his behavior. He should have been more considerate of my preferences instead of his own.

JAMES: Right.

Emily hypothesized that Nina moved too fast to solutions without understanding the couple's problem sequences. Then she sent Nina a message through Zoom and suggested she spend more time on learning about the problem sequences and validating each client's feelings and thoughts.

NINA: Okay, let's step back. If I understand correctly, Charlotte, you got angry because James chose a restaurant that you did not like, and it did not meet your expectations. Your anger was intensified when he apologized because you were not sure if he understood why you were angry. Is that correct?

CHARLOTTE: Yes, that's pretty much it.

NINA: Great. James, can you tell me more about what was going on with you when you saw Charlotte get angry? Where were your thoughts and feelings at that moment?

JAMES: I mentioned I process things slowly. When she got angry, I froze. I got overwhelmed and did not know what to say. Saying sorry is the only way I thought could help.

NINA: I see. You were saying that you did not know how to respond to her anger at that moment. Did you understand her anger?

JAMES: I saw this Indian restaurant newly open nearby our place and wanted to check it out. I forgot the fact that she disliked Indian food. Yes, I got why she was angry. But it only came to my mind a few minutes later.

NINA: So, at that moment when you did not know what to say, you felt compelled to apologize even though you did not know why Charlotte was angry.

JAMES: (turns to the therapist): Yes, I wanted to comfort her.

CHARLOTTE: (turns to James): That's exactly why I don't like your response. You either don't say anything or just apologize insincerely.

NINA: Charlotte, what were you thinking when you were angry?

CHARLOTTE: He did not care about me. That's why he ignored my preferences when booking the restaurant.

NINA: (summarizes the problem sequence): So, this may be your interactional pattern. Charlotte gets angry about something, and James does not respond immediately because he does not know the reason for her anger. James needed more time to think it through. To ease Charlotte's feeling of anger, James would apologize to Charlotte. Then Charlotte was more frustrated because she did not feel understood and cared for.

(Charlotte and James nodded.)

NINA: Did this interaction pattern happen on other occasions too?

CHARLOTTE: Yes, when we have sex, sometimes I get upset because he does not respond to what I want him to do. When I was trying to communicate more about it, he got more distant, and then we stopped.

After the live session ended, Emily and Nina had a debrief.

EMILY: You summarized the problem sequence well in the session. Is there anything else you want to add?

NINA: Charlotte had individual therapy for years. She has an extensive vocabulary about thoughts and feelings. She expects James to answer quickly and honestly. James is afraid of annoying her. And it takes him a longer time to process what happens. When she is looking for a quick answer, James says something that he thinks she wants to hear. Charlotte perceives it as dishonesty and presses him more. James withdraws to avoid confrontation.

EMILY: You have the key points. I agree. I think because James is a slow processor, at times he may feel intimidated by Charlotte's intense expressiveness. Did you notice that Charlotte interrupted him several times in the session? What do you think can be a solution sequence?

NINA: Yes, I did notice that. I agree that is part of their problem sequence. If Charlotte can allow James to have extra time to process his responses without interrupting or blaming him, and James can honestly ask Charlotte to give him more time to think, that can be a solution.

EMILY: It makes sense. In the next session, you can talk more about a solution sequence. Now let's step back. What did you think about my suggestions during your live session?

NINA: Yes, I agree with you. I think I went too fast because I knew you were watching. I have not been watched by former supervisors. And I felt the pressure to do something to show you that I can implement IST.

EMILY: Understood. It is normal that you feel nervous being observed. And you are new to IST. You are doing an excellent job. Do you think your clients are on board with you about the definition of the problem sequence?

NINA: I think so. I checked in with them about my hypothesis and they verbally confirmed it, and I can also tell from their body language.

EMILY: That's great. Sometimes it takes longer for clients to fully comprehend their problem sequence. They may appear to agree with your hypothesis in the session and go back to their regular problematic interactions in real life with little awareness. Therefore, it is helpful for therapists to repeat the problem sequence in different sessions to deepen their self-awareness. There are signs that the clients digest the systemic idea of a problem sequence. These are when clients can refer to their interactions as a pattern, and when they can analyze their own behaviors and how they contribute to the pattern. How you proceed will depend on your evaluation of their understanding of the problem sequence. You will only move towards generating a solution sequence when you feel that they have a good understanding of the problem sequence and want to change it. Let's discuss more next time.

As seen in this vignette, it is important to teach therapists how to collaborate with the clients to locate the problem in a problem sequence by tracking it in detail, formulating and communicating a formulation of it to the clients, and seeking clients' feedback as per the IST blueprint. These skills may come naturally for some therapists and need more in-depth work with others. Some therapists may find it difficult to present their formulation of the sequence (hypothesis) directly to clients as they don't feel comfortable doing so or they were previously trained to offer minimum input to clients. Locating the problem in a problem sequence facilitates clients' systemic conceptualization of their presenting problems and prevents them from blaming themselves or others. When the clients are not ready to view the problem in a problem sequence, the therapist may feel frustrated and impatient. The supervisor validates the therapist's frustration in an encouraging way and redirects them to try alternative ways of conversing with clients about the problem. For example, it may help to review multiple incidents of the problem unfolding to help the client see the pattern's repetitive nature. The supervisor also nurtures the therapist's enthusiasm in learning and practicing IST. Therefore, the supervisor's ability to conduct the conversation in a positive, warm, and constructive way is crucial to help their therapists build confidence, find acceptance of where the clients are at, and develop conversing competence to guide the clients to move forward. Chapter 6 includes additional discussion of therapist development of skills in conversing and reading feedback.

Step 3: Identifying a Solution Sequence

Once the supervisor has helped the therapist locate the problem sequence, the next step is to identify a solution sequence. The supervisor encourages the therapist to consider solution sequences from multiple sources, including "common-sense knowledge about how to solve problems, knowledge of best practices about how to handle difficult situations, empirically supported findings from models of therapy that address particular problems or situations, and the therapist's previous experience with similar situations" (Pinsof et al., 2018, p. 64). The following vignette is provided to illustrate the process of helping therapists identify a solution sequence.

Vignette

Jessica, a White therapist in her late 20s, graduated from the Marriage and Family Therapy program where Emily served as adjunct faculty. Since Emily was her supervisor during the program and she wanted to resume IST supervision, Jessica hired Emily as her supervisor even though she had obtained licensure.

Jessica consulted with Emily about a family with an identified client named Madelyn, an eight-year-old Latina girl. Madelyn showed anxiety and defiant behaviors at home with her parents and siblings. Her mother, Lydia, was 35 years old and works as a nurse. Her father, Alejandro, was 37 years old and worked in construction. He recently took a new job and often traveled for work. Madelyn had a ten-year-old brother named Martin and a five-year-old sister named Julie. The family lived together with Lydia's 60-year-old mother, Krystal, whose husband died two years ago. Lydia was overwhelmed with taking care of the three children. Krystal provided child-care support to Lydia.

Jessica had been working with the family, including both parents and Madelyn, for six months. Due to his busy travel schedule, Alejandro attended sessions occasionally.

EMILY: What are your thoughts about the problem sequence?

JESSICA: Based on my assessment, as well as my communication with the siblings' therapists, the primary issue is the inconsistency in the parent subsystem regarding parenting behaviors and parental conflicts. Alejandro and Lydia were never married, and they had an on-and-off relationship in the last three years. They broke up at one point and they got back together later. Although Alejandro is now back in the family, he is still absent most of the time due to work. I only met him once in the intake session. He sees his role as that of a provider, and he shows love to the children through giving gifts. The three children lack a consistent and competent parental subsystem. When Alejandro comes back home after weeks of traveling, he and Lydia often argue because they have different parenting values and therefore parenting practices. Lydia's parents came from Costa Rica, but she grew up in New York State. Lydia had an indulgent parenting style, and she did not set up rules for the children to follow. Alejandro originally came from Puerto Rico, and he was raised with an authoritarian parenting style to which he still felt committed. He is a strict father who has high expectations for his children.

EMILY: I am glad that you communicated with the other two children's therapists. Is there an issue that is common to the three children?

JESSICA: Yes, the children sometimes witnessed the parents' verbal arguments over parenting practices. I think they did not know whose rules to follow.

EMILY: This case seems a good example of having multiple problem sequences of different durations. As you know, those four types are distinguished based on the length of time it takes the sequence to go through its cycle. Sequence 1 (S1s) are brief face-to-face interactions which last for seconds to hours. S2s are daily/weekly routines which last for one day to one week. S3s involve ebbs and flows of condition or problem that have a periodicity of between several weeks to a year or more. S4s are transgenerational patterns across two or more generations. Are you able to identify problem sequences of different durations in this case?

JESSICA: Okay. Let me try. I can tell that there is an S1 of Lydia's parenting interactions with the children that occurs when Alejandro is gone, and then there is an S3 defined by Alejandro's being away and then returning and imposing his discipline style.

EMILY: Perfect! I think these two sequences together make up the problem sequence and account for the anxiety of the children. What do you think?

JESSICA: Yes, now I see it.

Although IST does not require a careful review of each hypothesizing metaframework before the therapist and family construct a solution sequence, Emily decides to ask Jessica to reflect on each of the metaframeworks to create a learning experience and to facilitate a careful search for factors that may influence the solution sequence.

EMILY: What are your thoughts about the parental subsystem? What concepts from the hypothesizing metaframeworks did you observe?

JESSICA: The first idea that came to my mind is the organization hypothesizing metaframeworks. Because Alejandro was not in the picture of the family until recently, and Lydia experienced depression and chose a lenient parenting style, there is no strong leadership in the parental subsystem. In the parent-child subsystem, there is a lack of hierarchy between Lydia and the three children. Because Lydia does not set rules, the children do not respect her much as a parent.

EMILY: I agree with this hypothesis. What is Krystal's role in the parental subsystem? Does she intervene when they have conflicts? What kind of parenting style does she have?

JESSICA: Krystal helps with childcare especially when Lydia is at work, but she does not do much when Alejandro and Lydia have conflicts. Her style of parenting is like that of her daughter, Lydia. She does not establish rules and believes children should do whatever they want to be happy. That's how she parented Lydia.

EMILY: Got it. How about any other hypothesizing metaframeworks?

JESSICA: I guess it would be gender. Alejandro plays the role of a provider, and he does not want to get involved in day-to-day childrearing activities. He believes those are women's responsibilities. When he gets back home from work, he is too tired to do anything with the kids.

EMILY: How about Lydia? Does she agree with Alejandro's belief about gender roles?

JESSICA: Not really. She complained that she worked as well, and it was too much for her to handle three kids. She stresses out when the children act out and don't listen to her direction.

EMILY: Great. What else? How about culture?

JESSICA: That's a good point. Yes, because Alejandro and Lydia grew up in different cultures, and the cultural differences may contribute to their different parenting values.

EMILY: Good. Yes, I think there may be greater specificity in those cultural differences that you will need to explore. How about development?

JESSICA: I haven't thought about it.

EMILY: Let me explain. Madelyn has been in the developmental stage that includes learning how to take responsibility. Because both Lydia and Krystal did not set up clear expectations for Madelyn's responsibilities, Madelyn did not have opportunities to learn certain skills and develop self-management abilities which may contribute to her anxiety.

JESSICA: Makes sense. Thank you.

EMILY: My pleasure. We have discussed a lot about problem sequences. Let's talk about the next step—constructing a solution sequence. What's your hypothesis about this?

JESSICA: Now, after we talked through the problem sequence, a solution sequence is clearer to me. The parents need to work together. Alejandro needs to be more involved in Madelyn's life so she can feel cared for. Lydia and Alejandro need to understand their differences in parenting values and styles, and figure out a consistent way to set up rules, express love to their children, and discipline them. Madelyn needs to feel that her parents are on the same team.

EMILY: You suggest a very reasonable set of solution sequences. And, yes, it would be ideal if Madelyn had a chance to tell her parents how she felt and what she hoped to get from them.

JESSICA: Yes, Madelyn feels powerless in the family. It would be great if she could express her worry to her parents, especially her dad.

EMILY: Agreed. My guess is that Alejandro may not know how to play other aspects of fatherhood in addition to the role of provider. He may need more help so he can step up and take on more responsibilities.

JESSICA: Okay. I will work with the family to collaborate to create a solution as we have just discussed. I will help the parents understand more about Madelyn's concern and help them to be on the same page with parenting practices. Do I need to ask them more about their relationship?

EMILY: Not at this moment, especially when Madelyn is present in therapy. You want to focus on their co-parenting relationships for now because they are directly related to the presenting problem of Madelyn's anxiety and defiant behaviors. If you have a better alliance with them and you believe it is beneficial to explore their relationship considering the mental health condition of Madelyn, you can do that later. The next step will be to present your plan for solution sequences to the family and tie the changes you are suggesting directly to their concerns about Madelyn and to the problem sequences you have identified. With their agreement, you can begin to work on the specific solution sequences.

Because Jessica was an advanced therapist who had considerable experience working with families and had received IST supervision, the supervisor intentionally stepped back and encouraged Jessica to think about the solution sequence. Her communication with Jessica was more direct than how she talked with less experienced therapists. On a separate note, it is not uncommon that therapists see many issues in the client system as problematic and they want to fix everything. This poses a risk for them to lose focus, and it may distract them from the clients' presenting concerns which can threaten the therapeutic alliance. In other words, the supervisor must help the therapist determine which problem sequences are most germane to the presenting problem and focus their interventions on them.

Step 4: Implementing the Solution Sequence

Compared to other steps in the essence diagram, implementing the solution sequence is straightforward. The detailed explanations can be found in Russell et al. (2023). However, because therapists may assume that the client knows how to do the new sequence, they may not spend enough time setting up its implementation. The supervisor reminds therapists to discuss a concrete plan with the client system about how to implement it. The following questions are important for the therapist to consider: Should I ask the clients to implement the solution sequence in the therapy session or outside of therapy? Are they ready to implement the solution sequence? Does the client system have sufficient skills to implement the solution sequence? What can the therapists do to ensure that the client system knows what exactly each of them needs to do and how to do it? What will the therapist do if one or more individuals in the client system seem ambivalent about the solution sequence or refuse to implement it? Without a thoughtful plan, the implementation is highly likely to fail, and the client system will feel disappointed, discouraged, and frustrated.

Vignette

Jacob was a graduate student in the last semester of his Marriage and Family Therapy program. He worked with a family that included the mother, Jacklyn (30 years old), and two children, Edison (six years old), and

Liam (eight years old). This was a mixed-race family of low socioeconomic status. Jacklyn and Edison lived together. Jacklyn had two marriages that ended in divorce. Edison and Liam had different biological fathers, each of whom was involved in co-parenting activities. Jacklyn was Latina. Edison's father, Eon, was Black. Edison, the identified client, visited Eon weekly. Liam recently resided with his father Daniel, who is White, in another state but will return in two months. Jacklyn had good co-parenting relationships with the children's fathers, Eon and Daniel. Jacklyn was the primary care-giver for the two boys, and she worked as a caregiver earning less than $30K a year. Jacklyn had a family history of depression (maternal grandmother), schizophrenia (mother), and bipolar (uncle and brother). Jacklyn sought therapy for Edison because she was worried about Edison's outbursts of extreme emotion and dramatic thoughts. She was afraid these were early signs of mental health problems.

Jacob had identified a problem sequence and solution sequence. He consulted with Emily, his supervisor, on how to help clients implement a solution sequence.

JACOB: The direct client system includes Jacklyn, Edison, and Liam. The indirect client system includes Edison's father, Eon, Jacklyn's boyfriend, Karl, and Liam's father, Daniel. Edison's father, Eon, has not been available to attend sessions so far, but I hope to involve him in the future. I have not invited Jacklyn's boyfriend, Karl, now because he does not live in the house and is not involved in daily activities.

EMILY: Sounds reasonable to me. What is the problem sequence and solution sequence you have identified?

JACOB: The problem sequence involves a series of events that occur between Edison and Jacklyn around bedtime. Edison usually plays with his tablet at bedtime. Edison recently has had nightmares and disturbing dreams which wake him up at night. When Edison wakes, he wakes Jacklyn, disturbs her sleep, and refuses to return to his room. Jacklyn and I agreed that screen time prevented Edison from getting ready for bed, and the interactions in the night between him and Jacklyn further interrupted sleep for both of them. The solution sequence I came up with was for Jaclyn to establish a routine for Edison, including enga-ging in physical activities at least three hours before bed, and playing soothing music in the evening, and to do something restful prior to bedtime. Restful activity is meant to replace screen time as evidence shows that screen time before bed can interrupt one's sleep. Jacklyn would put Edison to bed. At the same time, Jacklyn and I will teach Edison the differences between dreams and reality through reading some children's books together. If he wakes Jacklyn up, Jacklyn will reassure him and direct him back to his room to sleep.

EMILY: Did Jacklyn and Edison agree with this plan?

JACOB: I think Jaclyn agreed but she had some hesitations.

EMILY: What is her concern?

JACOB: When Edison wakes Jacklyn up, Jacklyn foresees that she will have a tough time putting Edison back in his room because he would try everything to stay in her room. It would become a battle and Jacklyn would give up easily.

EMILY: I am glad that Jacklyn felt comfortable sharing her concern with you. It provides you with a chance to think through every step of the implementation. How will you address her concern?

JACOB: I've no idea. I do not have lots of experience working with children. Jacklyn is stressed out after the interruption of her sleep. However, I understand that she wants to comfort Edison and finds it hard to leave him alone.

EMILY: Yeah. It is not unusual for kids at this age to have bad dreams. It is also difficult for parents to be consistent with the bedtime routine. I think you have already done an excellent job identifying a solution sequence that can really help with Edison's sleep. Did Jacklyn think about having a stuffed animal as company for Edison? You or she can introduce this animal as a friend who, like his mother, can protect Edison from any monsters. After Edison develops a relationship with this stuffed animal, he may not reach out to Jacklyn as much. Or if Edison goes to Jacklyn's room, Jacklyn can send him back with the animal. I am just thinking about a replacement.

JACOB: I have not thought about it. But I will discuss this possibility with them.

EMILY: Great. The key is to find a method that both Jacklyn and Edison feel confident to try.

JACOB: Understood. I will let you know how things are going next week.

EMILY: Great.

As shown in the vignette, implementing solution sequences often requires the client to have changes in their cognitive, behavioral, and/or emotional responses which can be the opposite of what they usually do. Changing someone's habits and natural tendencies takes time. The therapist can be easily upset if the implementation does not go well. In addition to making sure that the therapist goes through all the details that are involved in the implementation with clients, the supervisor also normalizes the therapist's reactions if things do not go as planned. In IST, failure is welcomed in therapy and in supervision as it presents the opportunity to gain a better understanding of the constraints and shift the work to address them. Solution sequences are experiments that either find success or identify additional information that facilitates problem-solving. The supervisor can model this attitude to their therapists by acknowledging their own mistakes with the hope that the therapist can communicate to their clients that any new initiatives or efforts are commendable and experimental, and failures can help find fresh solutions.

Step 5: Evaluate Outcome

After the clients agree to implement a solution sequence, the next step is to evaluate the outcome of it. The evaluation is a collaboration between the therapist and the client. Although it is common for therapists to begin a session by checking in with the client about how their last week went or on homework progress, those conversations are usually brief and informal. Evaluating the outcome of the implementation of a solution sequence requires more careful planning and attention to detail. The supervisor focuses on the therapist's process of evaluation rather than the result. To begin with, the supervisor simply asks the therapist, "How did it go?" just the same as the therapist may ask their client. Other questions that can be asked by the supervisor include: "What was the client's response?", "How did you engage the clients in this conversation?", "Were you able to help them fully describe what they did and didn't do?", "Do you feel the process went smoothly?", "How did the clients react to their attempt at the solution sequence?", and "What was it like for you to hear about their efforts and the outcome?" Regardless of the outcomes, the evaluation of the implementation will always bring valuable data and opportunities for growth.

The necessity and timing of the evaluation need to be highlighted in supervision. Some therapists may be hesitant to ask clients about the results of attempting solution sequences because they are worried that little or no progress was made. Therapists may skip evaluating the implementation and continue to passively listen to the client's problem-saturated stories. This happens often with therapists at an early stage of their development, whereas experienced therapists may feel more comfortable asking clients about the solution sequence. When there is a task for the client to do that the therapist does not follow up on, the task may never be completed. The risk is that the client will not take any future therapy tasks seriously. Over time, the client and therapist will feel defeated when they notice no progress. Therefore, the supervisor expresses their expectation that the therapist will follow up with clients on the outcome of the implementation of solution sequences. When the supervisor notices the therapist is reluctant to do so, they need to ask the therapist to explore the constraints that keep them from carefully following up. The supervisor can validate the therapist's fear and coach the therapist to have an open mind to any responses that they may receive from the client. The supervisor emphasizes the failure-driven principle and helps the therapist appreciate what can be learned from the outcome with the hope that the therapist will bring this attitude to their clients.

When the Implementation Is Successful

If the implementation is successful, the supervisor highlights what the therapist has done and compliments their ability in specific areas. The supervisor can say something like "It feels good to hear positive progress. Can we spend some time reviewing what you have done that contributed to it?" The therapist will hopefully feel validated and encouraged by the supervisor who serves as a witness to their growth in developing solution sequences. Following that, the supervisor helps the therapist to plan how to positively reinforce the client's improvement in therapy. If the clients do the sequence consistently and it significantly improves the problem, then the essence diagram bypasses some of the steps and goes directly to Step 8—implement and maintain the solution sequence.

When the Implementation Is Not Successful

While positive outcomes are celebrated and reinforced, the supervisor helps the therapist to process and embrace undesirable outcomes using the failure-driven guideline. If the implementation does not go well, it becomes an opportunity to learn more about the client system and its constraints. While the failure-driven principle reduces anxiety in dealing with failure, the IST essence and blueprint provide a practical guide for what to do when failure happens.

There are different specific outcomes when the implementation is not successful. The client system may not try it at all although they agree to do so. The client system may try it a few times and give up quickly. Another outcome is that the client system performs the solution sequence, but it does not lead to improvement in the presenting problem. The supervisor works with the therapist to identify constraints when encountering each of those circumstances. More discussions about how to address these different outcomes can be found in Step 6—identify the constraints.

In parallel, the supervisor is also evaluating the outcome of supervision which is mostly related to the therapist's clinical competence. The supervisor may manage feelings of frustration or discouragement when the therapist reports little therapy progress. They may have doubts about their clinical competence in general or specifically related to IST. This applies to both inexperienced and experienced therapists. The supervisor avoids harsh criticism and instead validates the therapist's efforts and shows acceptance, support, and warmth regardless of the outcomes. To do that, the key is to understand that there are many complex factors impacting the outcomes of implementing a solution sequence. Examples of those factors are inaccurate hypothesis about the problem sequence and solution sequence, bad timing for the implementation of the solution sequence, or other unexpected barriers that the therapist and client system encounter. There are equally complex factors on the therapist's side (e.g., self-of-the-therapist issues, stage of development as a therapist) that can decrease their capacity to facilitate the evaluation effectively. For evaluating supervision outcomes, the supervisor needs to consider the therapist's developmental needs and reflect on their training priorities and personal values. When the supervisor is patient and highlights the therapist's strengths and growth and accepts mistakes and limitations, this view and attitude can be transferred to the therapy room.

THE SUPERVISOR: I understand you hope to see progress with your clients, as all of us do. When there isn't any progress, you may be feeling incompetent and have self-doubts. You may doubt whether you can be a good therapist. You may doubt whether you conduct IST in the right way. Those thoughts are normal. But I want to distinguish something here. If your client fails to implement the solution sequence, it only means that more work is needed. You and the client will work together to figure it out using the IST essence and blueprint. As a systemic thinker, you know that things happen in contexts. Failure does too. Experiencing failure is a normal part of human lives and a perfect moment to identify constraints that keep the solution sequence from being implemented. That's what I love about IST. It helps you to change perspectives about failure and hopefully change your client's perspectives too. There are many reasons for a lack of successful implementation. It may be because the hypothesis is inaccurate. You can work with the client to revise it. The solution sequence could be good in theory, but there are other implementation barriers you and the client had not thought about. Or maybe the timing is not ideal. Your client may need more time or preparation to be ready to implement it. Change is not easy for a lot of people. You are doing an excellent job of moving through the first few steps of the IST essence. Let us work together to understand more about what happened.

Step 6: Identify the Constraints

When the above evaluation indicates that the clients did not successfully implement the solution sequence, the supervisor helps the therapist identify the constraints to the implementation. Constraints can be identified from one or a combination of the hypothesizing metaframeworks. They can also come from other areas such as the client's readiness to change, a lack of insight and awareness of their patterns, and a key member's unwillingness to attend therapy. Anything that keeps the client stuck in their old problem sequence can be a constraint. The question "What prevents you from doing what you had planned to do?" seems simple and easy to ask. It is important for the supervisor to process what the client's responses mean to the therapist. In addition to teaching the therapist to ask constraint questions and interpret the feedback, the supervisor also encourages the therapist to develop their own hypotheses about constraints and make decisions about when and how to share these hypotheses with the clients.

There are different scenarios when the implementation is not successful. The client system may not try it at all although they agree to do so. Various constraints may contribute to their lack of action. Some clients may describe that they did not have a chance to implement the solution sequences due to a busy schedule or a lack of confidence. Clients' answers to the therapist's question can be short—for example, "I got busy and forgot about it." For those clients, the supervisor needs to encourage the therapist to further explore the client's busy schedule and re-examine whether the solution sequence is feasible. At the same time, the supervisor guides the therapist to not take what the client says about their busy schedule at a face value. Is it about their schedule or are there other constraints involved? For clients who are constrained by worry they will not do it "right," the therapist can explain the win-win nature of experiments. Both success and failure advance problem-solving. Welcoming failure as a chance to advance problem-solving can reduce fear and shame associated with not doing it "right" the first time. Another example is that one or more members may agree on the plan in session whereas their conflicts during the week prevent them from being willing to try the solution sequence. Clients may say, "I wanted to do it, but we had another argument this week. I was discouraged. What is the point of making this effort?" This reveals another problem sequence in the imple-mentation process: clients' weekly arguments (Sequence 2) constrain their ability to implement the solution sequence. In this case, it is important to encourage the therapist to share this hypothesis with the client at an appropriate time.

Some clients may try it and quickly give up when the implementation does not work. They may say, "I tried, and I was discouraged by my family's responses, and I stopped." In this case, the supervisor helps the therapist understand the interaction between the client and their family members, and hypothesizes how the clients can respond differently to each other. Other clients may encounter challenges and events that they and the therapist have not thought about. For instance, a client underestimates the challenges of being in an interracial relationship and the impact of their partner's experi-ences of racism on their relationship. Another client may not recognize how sexual trauma influences their current sex life. An immigrant family may not comprehend how their lack of social, cultural, financial, and familial resources limits their support for treating their son's autism disorder. In those cases, training the therapist to be sensitive to the hypothesizing meta-frameworks can help them develop a deep awareness of the multi-dimensional nature of human life and the intersectionality within a social, political, economic, and cultural context.

To become proficient at identifying constraints, the therapist first needs to understand, with the guidance of the supervisor, what each of the hypothesizing metaframeworks entails. The supervisor can provide examples from their clinical experiences to facilitate comprehension. When a therapist either lacks the knowledge of or first-hand experiences with any of the seven metaframeworks, they will need more coaching from the supervisor in addition to resources such as readings, movies, museums, interactions with people from other cultures and religious traditions, and training. For example, a male therapist does not have an in-depth understanding of how gender socialization impacts mental health and relationships in a patriarchal society. By opening the gender metaframework, the supervisor can enhance his awareness of the potential power difference in a heterosexual relationship that may constrain his ability to discuss gender roles and inequality existing in the partners' household chores division, financial decisions, and childrearing values. A heterosexual cisgender therapist may ignore their biases towards the sexual and gender minority populations and not recognize the unique challenges and strengths these populations have. The supervisor can use the culture metaframework to strengthen the therapist's competence in these areas of knowledge. A therapist who is born and grew up in another country may not understand how educational systems work in the United States (or a different country). This may prevent the therapist from helping clients find the support and resources for their children who struggle academically or socially at school. A therapist compares themselves with a more experienced therapist and feels inadequate. They do not fully appreciate their differences in developmental stages. A racially minoritized therapist feels that they are inferior to their White clients, which prevents them from sharing their expertise and knowledge with the clients. A therapist who is an atheist may not recognize the positive and negative impact of clients' spiritual beliefs on the maintenance or resolution of the problem sequence. Notably, the seven metaframeworks are intersectional. The therapist must consider how the interactions of multiple factors contribute to the problem sequence, solution sequence, and constraints. The supervisor can ask the therapist, "Which hypothesizing metaframeworks seem relevant in identifying the constraints?"

Furthermore, it is important to highlight the value of social justice embedded in multiple hypothesizing metaframeworks. IST recognizes that disenfranchised client systems, due to their social locations in society, experience constraints related to a lack of access to power and resources (Pinsof et al., 2018). Therefore, the supervisor encourages the therapist to increase their cultural humility, show compassion, and advocate for clients as much as they can. The therapist is expected to develop the ability to work with diverse populations. To do that, the therapist takes the responsibility to access the local knowledge of clients' lives through education, reading, media, and personal life experiences.

Step 7: Attempt to Lift the Constraints

After the therapist identifies the constraints, the next task is to find concepts, strategies, and interventions drawn from the six planning metaframeworks to remove the constraints. The interventions of most therapy approaches are categorized into six domains that make up the planning metaframeworks. The planning metaframeworks begin with action-oriented interventions (e.g., enactments, behavioral exposure, behavioral activation) and proceed to meaning/emotion interventions (e.g., reframing, cognitive restructuring, externalization, accessing primary emotion) and biobehavioral interventions (e.g., exercise, relaxation exercises, psychotropic medication). These three planning metaframeworks provide interventions that focus on the present. When they are insufficient to lift constraints, three planning metaframeworks that address the past are indicated: the family-of-origin, internal representation, and self-planning metaframeworks. The order of use of the metaframeworks is not about the superiority of one over another, but rather how time-consuming each intervention is. Following the cost-effective guideline, therapists begin with brief, direct, and simple interventions before they move to more complicated and time-consuming interventions. The planning metaframeworks and their order of application are discussed in detail by Pinsof et al. (2018) and Russell et al. (2023).

The supervisor will need to help the therapist distinguish adopting a model from utilizing an intervention from a model. This is an important contribution of IST, that interventions from various approaches can be brought to bear on the various constraints that are discovered in each case. Therapists do not need to be loyal to a theory to use some interventions and techniques from the theory. For example, a therapist can use an "externalizing the problem" intervention from narrative therapy without identifying as a narrative therapist. As IST provides a theoretical map for integration, therapists have endless opportunities to learn and apply new interventions that have been developing in the field.

The structure of planning metaframeworks provides the therapist with a general understanding of how the concepts, strategies, and interventions from various therapy theories fit into each of the planning metaframeworks. For example, some interventions from behavioral approaches belong to the action planning metaframework, but others that focus on changing people's perceptions or emotions fit into the meaning/emotion planning framework. An extensive list of interventive strategies within each planning metaframework can be found in Pinsof et al. (2018) and Russell et al. (2023). The therapists may learn theories and interventions from their academic program, postgraduate training, workshops, conferences, readings, online resources, and supervision. The supervisor can play an educator's role by introducing some interventions. For instance, a supervisor helps the therapist understand and practice selected interventions from dialectical behavioral therapy (DBT; Linehan, 1987). Given time limitations, it is unrealistic for the supervisor to teach many interventions in detail, so the therapist will need to learn interventions from didactic courses or workshops as well. Their supervisor serves as a coach and helps therapists apply those skills in clinical practice within the IST framework. The conversation would be less about the therapy model and how to conceptualize the case through a particular therapy lens. It would be more about which interventions may be helpful to lift a constraint and implement a solution sequence. The supervisor can support the therapist's skills in choosing interventions by teaching them to utilize the blueprint's loop of hypothesizing, planning, conversing, and reading feedback.

Unlike a manualized treatment, IST provides the therapist flexibility and freedom to develop their own style based on their personality, preferences, values, and characteristics. Thus, the IST supervisor encourages the therapist to develop their unique style of conducting IST, which makes therapy personal and meaningful to them. The IST therapist can choose the interventions with which they want to build competencies without necessarily being limited by the theoretical assumptions of the original theory within which the interventions were developed. To implement the interventions from a specific model, the therapist does not have to train as practitioner of that model unless it is determined by the supervisor that it is necessary to do so. Regardless of what interventions the therapist chooses to use, the therapist needs to implement the interventions to a "good enough" degree (Russell & Breunlin, 2019). As an evaluator and gatekeeper, the supervisor must help their therapists develop their skills and evaluate whether they can deliver the intervention successfully and ethically. More experienced therapists who have developed skills in multiple therapy approaches have some advantages of easily accessing interventions with which they are familiar. They may need some assistance to ground these interventions within the IST framework.

Less experienced therapists establish competency with interventions one at a time and can continue over time to expand their capability to implement interventions from various approaches. Ideally, the therapist will soon comfortably use at least some interventions from each of the planning metaframeworks and produce effective treatment outcomes. The supervisor encourages the therapist to seek specialized training to implement some complex interventions from models in which the supervisor does not have expertise in (e.g., Internal Family Systems; Schwartz & Sweezy, 2019). The supervisor also discusses when to refer clients to another therapist when the therapist is constrained from implementing certain interventions necessary for the clients (e.g., EMDR; Shapiro, 2017).

According to the authors' observations, discussing how to implement an intervention can consume most of the time of a supervision meeting. Learning interventions that fit their clients' constraints brings a sense of comfort and confidence to the therapists because they feel that they are doing something helpful for the clients. It is important for the supervisor to validate their enthusiasm, but also remind them that implementing interventions is only one step of a complex therapy process. Without the context provided by the IST essence, blueprint, and guidelines including a strong therapeutic relationship, any intervention is likely to fall short. Therefore, the supervisor spends considerable time going through the decision-making process and helps the therapist understand which constraint they are targeting now and what interventions are appropriate to lift it.

Vignette

The following vignette is an example of implementing both Step 6 and Step 7, identifying, and attempting to lift a constraint.

Sue, a Black cisgender woman, was a therapist-in-training working at a local mental health agency following her recent graduation. She was supervised by Emily. Sue saw a family with a five-year-old son, Matthew, and an eight-month daughter, Aya, through an online platform. The father was Pedro, a cisgender Latino, who grew up in the United States, and the mother, Madeleine, was a cisgender woman who had immigrated to the US from Ireland with her parents. Pedro and Madelyn were both in their late 30s. The family's primary concern was Mathew's attention deficit hyperactivity disorder (ADHD). Madeleine, an occupational therapist, took major responsibility for Matthew's care, and she blamed Pedro for some of his parenting decisions. Pedro did not believe in Matthew's diagnosis and tended to minimize Matthew's behavioral challenges. Furthermore, he withdrew from parenting tasks and kept a distance from Matthew when Matthew showed aggressive behaviors. Pedro lacked confidence about being a father. They both felt exhausted taking care of their eight-month-old daughter, Aya. The parents sitting in the room suggested their family dynamics. Pedro sat alone in a chair holding Aya, while Madeleine sat with Matthew and interacted with him.

The problem sequence was that the parents were not on the same page about parenting a child with ADHD and they interacted with each other in a criticize–withdraw pattern that increased Madeleine's anxiety and reduced Pedro's confidence and involvement in co-parenting behaviors. The therapists and the clients came to an agreement that Madeleine would step back and give space for Pedro to take on family and parenting responsibilities. Further, they agreed that increasing Pedro's confidence in his parenting role would be an important part of strengthening the parental subsystem and providing a stable structure for the children. The solution sequence begins with reducing Madeleine's criticism and promoting Pedro's engagement in their communication. Another solution sequence is to provide psychoeducation that enhances Pedro's understanding of ADHD so he can have productive discussions with Madeleine and professionals about how to best help

Matthew reduce parenting stress. To implement the solution sequence, Sue coached the parents to do communication exercises including discussing their views on parenting and mental health. Although Madeleine did not use critical words, she often interrupted Pedro and spoke for him. At times Madeleine also interrupted the conversation between Sue and Pedro. In addition, Pedro was still distant from Matthew. After a few repetitive, unproductive conversations, Sue discussed progress with the clients, and they agreed that little progress had been made. Sue felt disappointed that she was not more helpful and had doubts regarding her ability to help the family.

In supervision, Emily noticed Sue's frustration when describing treatment progress. Emily engaged Sue in a supportive discussion of Sue's feelings of frustration and incompetence. Then Emily asked her what was preventing the parents from effective communication. Sue stated her wish for Madeleine to give up control and let Pedro participate more in the household and childcare. She struggled to understand why Madeleine was still so dominant in their conversations and household decision-making. Emily observed that Sue did not directly answer the "constraint" question. Instead, she seemed frustrated with the mother and possibly sided with the father. Emily shared her concern that there may be an unbalanced therapeutic alliance. Sue acknowledged that it was difficult for her to connect with Madeleine. Then Sue generated the hypothesis that this might increase Madeleine's need to interrupt her interactions with Pedro. Emily proposed that understanding more about the family's background and history may help Sue contextualize the parental interactions, identify constraints, and increase her empathy for Madeleine.

From the information gleaned by Sue in subsequent sessions, the supervisor hypothesized constraints conceptualized in terms of the organization, development, gender, and culture metaframeworks that may be keeping Madelyn and Pedro from having effective communication. Among them, gender and culture seemed to be two profound factors. Madeleine had an elevated level of anxiety about Matthew's ADHD related to her professional experiences as an occupational therapist and her role as the mother. As the oldest daughter in an immigrant family, because her parents were busy at work to support their living, she took on many family duties, including taking care of her younger sister who had autism. Given that she played a caregiver role for her sibling in her family of origin, the leadership patterns between the parental subsystem and child subsystem were reversed and the boundaries were diffuse. These aspects of family organization seemed to have been necessary for the family's adjustment back then. In her current family, it was difficult for her to step back and let Pedro handle Matthew and Aya and other family responsibilities. On the other hand, based on the gender roles he reported learning in his culture, Pedro thought women should oversee childrearing and his primary role should be that of provider. Yet he grew up in a low-income family in which his mother was the provider who worked multiple jobs to maintain a living. This instilled in Pedro a keen sense of financial responsibility for the family. Furthermore, the emphasis on masculinity as he understood it prevented him from showing vulnerable feelings such as feeling inadequate as a father. He grew up with a single mother and did not learn much about how to be a father who spends time with the kids and engages in many caregiving activities. For Pedro, the transition to parenthood was a difficult developmental task. Finally, although Pedro grew up in the US, mental health issues and their treatment were novel and even threatening to him. He shared that in his culture expressing mental health concerns is viewed as a weakness.

Emily shared her hypotheses about the clients' constraints with Sue. In particular, she pointed out the connection between each parent's gender socialization in their respective cultural contexts and their tendency to be engaged in gender-stereotyped parenting behaviors. Emily and Sue had a substantive conversation about the gender hypothesis that seemed to have advanced their alliance. However, growing up in a traditional household, Sue did not see how the couple's respective gender socializations were a constraint. To address Sue's lack of understanding of gender and cultural socialization, Emily assigned some readings and a video on gender socialization and feminism for Sue to review. Emily wondered about Sue's family-of-origin experience and its impact on her self-of-the-therapist with respect to gender but decided to begin with a straightforward educational approach. This is an example of hypothesizing, planning, and implementing strategies to address a therapist's constraint. After more discussions with Sue about the materials, the supervisor felt that Sue had acquired sufficient knowledge which transferred to her conceptualization of the constraints in this case. Sue reported an increase in her understanding of the impact of the gender and culture hypothesizing metaframeworks. In therapy, Sue carried on similar discussions with the family about the constraints. To remove those constraints, the supervisor suggested Sue use some concepts and interventions that come from the emotion/meaning planning framework. Specifically, the supervisor encouraged Sue to learn more about the concepts from feminist therapy such as egalitarian relationships as well as gender role and power analysis. It was not essential that Sue adopt a feminist therapy theoretical framework to use this intervention. Instead, the concepts are utilized in therapy through an IST lens—in other words, examining how they describe constraints to the problem sequence and the implementation of the solution sequence.

With the opportunity to watch Sue's therapy sessions through a one-way mirror, the supervisor provided specific directions about how to integrate these concepts and techniques in working with this family. After six sessions, Madeleine was able to talk more directly with Pedro about his role, and Pedro had responded with increased understanding of Madeleine and a willingness to share more parental responsibilities. Their criticism–withdraw pattern was very much improved in their daily life. Emily asked Sue about her plan if the solution sequences related to communication and role functioning were maintained. Sue's plan is to shift to psychoeducation about ADHD, help the client find external resources to understand it (e.g., join a support group for parenting with ADHD children), and develop more intentional parenting behaviors.

Step 8: Implement and Maintain the Solution Sequence

For each therapy goal within a case, after the constraints are removed, the therapist goes back to Step 5 and works with the client to evaluate whether they can now successfully implement the solution sequences that they had identified. If the answer is no, the therapist needs to go to Step 6 and identify yet other constraints. If additional constraints are identified, they too need to be lifted. All along, the supervisor encourages the therapist to validate the client's progress and discuss how they can maintain the solution sequence over time. Sometimes more practice and time are needed to consolidate the solution sequence. Once the therapist and the client system determine that the solution sequence is successfully implemented and maintained, they will discuss whether their initial goal has been met. When the goal is met, the therapist will shift the work to another goal, if there is one, and begin a new round of the IST essence. If there are no additional goals, the therapist will guide the work toward termination.

Assuming the implementation is successfully maintained, the client is likely to be more hopeful and relaxed. The supervisor can call the therapist's attention to changes in the client's facial expressions and body postures and to changes in their communication sequences. This feedback can be read as reassurance that the client feels they are on the right track. This feedback along with the reports of client's improvement support the therapist's sense of self-efficacy, which has a ripple effect on their confidence in working with other clients. The supervisor, of course, is pleased with the therapist's acquisition of new skills and self-efficacy.

During this phase, it is important to remind the therapist to have a detailed discussion with the client about what they did to address their problems and attribute the progress to the client's persistence and hard work. It sets the stage for the client to do what needs to be done to maintain the solution sequence. Similarly, the supervisor talks with the therapist about what they did to make a difference in the therapy and helps the therapist own their acquisition of new skills and confidence. Receiving positive feedback from the supervisor is meaningful to the therapist's development of professional identity, especially when they are learning and applying a new theory. The supervisor, who serves as a mentor and a role model, helps the therapist to be confident that they can be an effective therapist. At this stage, therapists often wonder when termination is indicated. Experienced therapists usually have a sense of this as they observe progress and read and interpret the client's verbal and nonverbal feedback.

Other signs a therapist may notice include when the sessions cover the same ground, when there is less of a problem focus, or when they just do not know what to talk about in therapy. The supervisor can ask the therapist a range of questions to determine if the client is ready for termination: "Do you think the client is able to implement the solution sequences without your help?", "Are there any foreseeable factors or events that may interrupt the continuation of the solution sequences?", "Do you have an evaluation with the client regarding whether their goals are met?", "Does the client have additional goals for therapy?", "What do the client and you think about their readiness to terminate therapy?", and "Is the client on the same page regarding termination?" When the client and the therapist reach a consensus that their goals have been met and there is no new goal, it is time to consider termination. The therapist can reduce the frequency of meetings before the termination, though some terminations happen quickly. In the termination phase, the therapist reviews what has been accomplished, and what changes the client made, helps the client identify their strengths and resources, and discusses what situations may bring them back to therapy. The therapist can choose to share what it is like to work with the client if they want to.

Some therapists may have difficulty bringing up the topic of termination due to their fear of clients' perceptions of being abandoned. Some therapists feel very sad about saying goodbye to their clients, especially after they have worked together for a long time. The supervisor normalizes the therapist's concerns and feelings, helps them plan for how to conduct such conversations, and shares their own termination stories if appropriate.

There are circumstances for unnatural termination—for example, a therapist changes internship, jobs, or location, or a client changes geographic location or encounters unanticipated life events. In these cases, the supervisor advises the therapist to make a termination plan that allows the client enough time to prepare for the transition. When the client requires further therapy, the therapist needs to develop a plan for transferring or referring the client to another therapist. Meanwhile, the supervisor checks in with the therapist about their feelings about termination under these circumstances. The therapist may feel a lack of closure compared to a natural termination when the client's goals are met. They may keep wondering how the client is doing, whether they are working with a good therapist, and whether they will get to the destination they seek.

A certain level of unknowingness always exists for natural termination as well, as the therapist can never predict the client's future. It can be more difficult for unnatural terminations, especially when the main reason for termination is related to the therapist's change in circumstances. In such cases, the therapist may feel guilty or responsible for the end of the therapy and worry about the client's welfare. The therapist may miss seeing the client even when the cause of termination is client-related.

The supervisor explores the therapist's emotions in the various scenarios described above and asks questions to better understand the therapist's emotions and the meanings they make about them. The supervisor can share their own stories of client termination and their vulnerable feelings or facilitate a peer discussion within group supervision to normalize, validate, and process the therapist's intense and complex feelings. When the therapist can talk through whatever they are experiencing, they will likely feel relieved and be more prepared to discuss and manage the feelings they will have about future terminations.

Supervision often ends when the therapist leaves an internship site, graduates from an academic program, or finishes their postgraduate clinical hours. The supervisor handles termination of the supervisory relationship in a manner that parallels termination in therapy, including reviewing progress (acquisition of competencies), highlighting strengths and growing edges (including self-of-the-therapist issues), and discussing future career plans. The critical difference is that even though the supervisory relationship ends, it will not prevent the supervisor and the therapist from remaining connected as colleagues.

References

Beck, J. S. (2011). *Cognitive behavior therapy, second edition: Basics and beyond.* Guilford Press.

Breunlin, D. C., & Jacobsen, E. (2014). Putting the "family" back into family therapy. *Family Process*, 53(3), 462–475. https://doi.org/10.1111/famp.12083.

Butler, A. C., Chapman, J. E., Forman, E. M., & Beck, A. T. (2006). The empirical status of cognitive-behavioral therapy: A review of meta-analyses. *Clinical Psychology Review*, 26(1), 17–31. https://doi.org/10.1016/j.cpr.2005.07.003.

Diamond, G. S., Diamond, G. M., & Levy, S. A. (2014). *Attachment-based family therapy for depressed adolescents.* American Psychological Association.

Diamond, G., Russon, J., & Levy, S. (2016). Attachment-based family therapy: A review of the empirical support. *Family Process*, 55(3), 595–610. https://doi.org/10.1111/famp.12241.

He, Y., Hardy, N., & Russell, W. (2021). Integrative systemic supervision: Promoting therapists' theoretical integration in systemic therapy. *Family Process*, 61(1), 58–75. https://doi.org/10.1111/famp.12667.

Linehan, M. M. (1987). Dialectical behavior therapy for borderline personality disorder: Theory and method. *Bulletin of the Menninger Clinic*, 51(3), 261.

Pinsof, W. M., Breunlin, D. C., Russell, W. P., Lebow, J. L., Rampage, C., & Chambers, A. L. (2018). *Integrative systemic therapy: Metaframeworks for problem solving with individuals, couples, and families.* American Psychological Association.

Russell, W. P., Breunlin, D. C., & Sahebi, B. (2023). *Integrative systemic therapy in practice: A clinician's handbook.* Routledge.

Russell, W. P., & Breunlin, D. C. (2019). Transcending therapy models and managing complexity: Suggestions from integrative systemic therapy. *Family Process*, 58 (3), 641–655. https://doi.org/10.1111/famp.12482.

Schwartz, R. C., & Sweezy, M. (2019). *Internal family systems therapy.* Guilford Press.

Shapiro, F. (2017). *Eye movement desensitization and reprocessing (EMDR) therapy: Basic principles, protocols, and procedures.* Guilford Press.

Chapter 4

Other Issues Pertinent to IST Supervision

Technology, Ethical Issues, and Evaluation of Supervision Outcomes

Following Chapter 3 which describes the essential methods of conducting IST supervision, this chapter covers other important topics including the use of technology in therapy and supervision, ethical, legal, and risk issues in supervision, and the evaluation of supervision outcomes.

Technology in Supervision

IST supervision occurs in a large social-economic-cultural context where one element is the use of technology. Although online training programs and tele-therapy existed before COVID-19, the pandemic brought teletherapy and supervision to the front line. A mixed-method study surveyed a sample of American Association for Marriage and Family Therapy (AAMFT) Approved Supervisors and marriage and family therapy supervisees (N = 48) for their views of conducting systemic supervision using telehealth (Mosley et al., 2022). The benefits include enhanced accessibility for therapists residing in rural areas. The most noted limitation, however, is poor internet connection and running into technological difficulties. When technology issues happen, it can interfere with people's engagement and lead to ethical problems. Participants reported concerns about less engagement and connection in telehealth supervision, particularly group supervision. Some direct quotes from the participants are "I do not believe that thoughts are shared as openly in virtual supervision, and I find that I have a hard time maintaining my attention when fellow peers in supervision are speaking" and "Therapists seem less invested in the supervision relationship, are less prepared for supervision, and seem to take less responsibility" (p. 9). Moreover, the participants recognized that supervisors may lack engagement due to in-home distractions.

A few practical suggestions can address the internet connection and technology issues (Wootton et al., 2020). The supervisor talks with the therapist regarding whether a video-based supervision is appropriate to meet the therapist's needs and whether both are competent at using a videoconferencing platform upon receiving necessary training. All those involved in the supervision agree to learn how to use the platform and troubleshoot common

DOI: 10.4324/9781003146841-4

technology issues through reading the manual or attending training. Meanwhile, the supervisor sets up realistic expectations about telehealth supervision by informing the therapist that they may feel different in virtual supervision compared to in-person contact. The supervisor seeks feedback from the trainee about how to help them adapt to an online learning environment.

The Strengths and Constraints of Online IST Supervision

IST supervision is defined as a meta-perspective of supervision that utilizes the IST's theoretical frameworks and practical guidelines to develop therapists' clinical competence in conducting individual, couple, and family therapy and promote their development. As is the case in any approach, there are some unique strengths and challenges in conducting IST supervision through telehealth.

IST has an interpersonal guideline that therapists should prioritize working within a relational context directly involving multiple people in the client system rather than an individual client. Telehealth helps the clients to overcome scheduling and transportation barriers and increases the likelihood that multiple family members can attend therapy simultaneously. Family members can join the videoconferencing calls from different rooms and locations. When carefully planned, it provides the possibility to connect family members when they physically separate—for example, long-distance relationships. Furthermore, working with families remotely offers the therapist an opportunity to observe the client system in their day-to-day living contexts (e.g., home). The client system is in its most natural and comfortable space, which helps the therapist observe and identify problem sequences. Furthermore, observing the client system in the home environment may help identify untapped resources that can be used to formulate and implement solution sequences. Also, IST has the empirically informed guideline that states the clinical practice must be continually informed with empirical research and scientific data to be maximally effective and efficient. Telehealth makes it convenient for the therapist to share online information with the client system and the supervisor to share online data with the therapist.

In terms of challenges, the therapist may find it difficult to engage and assess multiple family members on a telehealth platform, particularly when working with family members in families of young children. Telehealth limits the therapist's ability to read clients' facial expressions, body language, and interactional cues (Wrape & McGinn, 2019). The therapist may capture what the client system verbally says in session but not their nonverbal language entirely. When more than two people in the same room join sessions, the therapist may have a hard time seeing them clearly. When family members are in different rooms, it may prevent the therapist from assessing and facilitating their direct verbal and physical interactions with each other compared to in-person therapy where they can sit on the same couch. Therefore, telehealth may limit the therapist and the supervisor to assess the client system's problem sequence (including risk situations), especially their problem sequences in therapy sessions. Telehealth also limits the therapist's ability to receive and interpret the client system's nonverbal feedback and therefore compromise their capacity to adjust treatment plan due to the limited feedback. When young children are involved in the direct client system, they may be easily distracted by their home environment, which surely interrupts the therapy process.

The supervisor should have a thorough discussion with the therapist about telehealth's strengths and limitations. The therapist's developmental needs, the policies of the academic program, agency, or private practice where they work, and the populations they serve need to be considered in this conversation. The supervisor evaluates the therapist's competency in being present in online therapy sessions and their troubleshooting abilities when encountering technology issues. Although some limitations are inevitable due to the nature of telehealth, a few practical suggestions are presented to increase the accuracy of assessment and feedback. The supervisor can suggest the therapist use multiple methods to collect information in order to conduct a comprehensive assessment. For instance, outcome measures can easily be sent to the client system to fill out prior to and during therapy sessions to both monitor the progress of therapy and collect feedback about the therapeutic alliance. The therapist can bring the results to therapy for discussion with clients. The supervisor also encourages the therapist to video-record their sessions or do live supervision so that another professional can also view their sessions and provide opinions.

When the therapist provides telehealth to high-risk populations with suicidal ideation/attempts, self-harm behaviors, domestic violence, and child abuse, the supervisor constantly assesses the therapist's ability and comfort level to provide adequate care. They also examine their own ability to handle crisis circumstances remotely through tele-supervision and how it can be done. To engage young children in a family context, the supervisor asks the therapist to seek additional reading and training (e.g., online interactive play therapy interventions) in providing online therapy to children and families.

When any technology is involved, there is a possibility of a lack of access or technology failures which can become a constraint. It can happen within the client system or the therapist system. It is possible that the client system has limited internet access or device (e.g., smartphone, laptop, tablet) access, particularly for disadvantaged clients. The client system may switch devices during therapy—for example, from a Zoom meeting on their laptop to a phone call. And the therapist may completely lose the client during therapy when technology fails. The supervisor reminds the therapist to be accommodating and flexible when the client system experiences technology problems. The therapist helps the client system find resources to address the lack of access and/or technology issues.

Supervisory Alliance in Online IST Supervision

To build supervisory alliance in online IST supervision, in the initial meeting, the supervisor must discuss in detail with the therapist about their expectations and limitations of online supervision. The supervisor shares the expectation for the therapist to be prepared, present, and engaged when attending supervision. In group supervision, because it is difficult to pick up social cues in a virtual space, the supervisor establishes a structure with operating rules to make sure everyone feels heard, has an equal share of time, and shares responsibilities for providing feedback to their peers. It may be helpful to explicitly talk about the meanings of nonverbal languages in an online environment to avoid misunderstanding.

The supervisor can ask questions to initiate discussions, such as "How comfortable are you with connecting with me online?", "What can I do to increase your trust and the effectiveness of online supervision?", "Do you want to meet with me fully virtually or do you want to do a hybrid format with some supervision sessions online and some supervision sessions in person?", "How confident are you that virtual supervision can meet your supervision goal which involves learning about how to practice therapy through the IST lens?", and "Do you have any concerns about receiving IST supervision remotely?"

Throughout the supervision, the supervisor must be mindful of how having virtual supervision impacts their own level of warmth, authenticity, articulation, empathy, and concentration. The supervisor wants to avoid distractions and interruptions in their work environment and ensure confidentiality in their private space. The supervisor may adjust their style working with therapists remotely, including talking more slowly, communicating more deliberately, and elevating their facial and verbal expressions to appear more visible. Like the therapist, the supervisor collects feedback from the therapist or multiple therapists in group supervision in multiple formats. The supervisor asks specific questions about their supervisory alliance and how the online supervision meets the therapist's goals both verbally and through sending questionnaires. The supervisor processes them with the therapist.

Ethical, Legal and Risk Issues

The supervisor serves as a gatekeeper to make sure that the therapist adheres to the state laws, agency policies, and profession's ethics. Some ethical, legal, and risk issues are discussed in the above section on technology use. IST supervision shares many similar concerns about ethical, legal, and risk issues with almost all the psychotherapy practice, such as responsibility to clients, responsibility to students and therapists, confidentiality, professional competence, and integrity. In addition, there are specific considerations about potential ethical, legal, and risk situations when conducting IST supervision. Four topics that are most relevant to IST supervision are explained in this section, including meeting the requirement of the profession and work setting, risk issues, changing therapy context, and relational ethics.

Meeting the Requirements in the Therapist's Profession/Work Setting

IST supervision aims to develop the therapist's clinical competence in conducting individual, couple, and family therapy and promote their development through using the IST framework. Each mental health profession has its own definition of clinical competence. While facilitating the therapist's ability to utilize IST tools for treatment conceptualization and delivery, the supervisor wants to make sure that the supervision helps the therapist meet the specific requirements of their profession and licensure, including their defined clinical competence, therapist development, and ethical guideline. The first question is whether the supervisor has the adequate qualifications (e.g., license in a certain mental health profession, approved supervisor credential) to provide supervision to particular therapists. Then the next question is whether the IST supervision can mostly address the core competencies defined by the therapist's profession and follow the local state laws and policies and expectations of their work settings. While evaluating whether IST supervision is a good fit for professions or work settings, the supervisor analyzes both the overlaps and differences between them. Not all mental health professions focus on training systemic therapists. However, they are mostly likely to welcome the idea of training integrative therapists. Some mental health agencies have specialty in certain therapy approaches (e. g., CBT or DBT). They are less likely to restrict their therapists to only practice these approaches, though. In this case, IST supervision can still be provided with a supplemental goal of helping the therapist gain competence in utilizing interventions from these specific approaches. The supervisor can check the specific requirement, communicate with the therapist and the staff in their professional organization, and consult the therapist's work setting (e.g., academic program, mental health agencies, private practice) and other supervisors in the same profession. This is especially important when handling crisis situations and ethical dilemmas, and helping the therapist in their licensure preparation because different professions and programs may have different guidelines.

Russell et al. (2023) have detailed discussions how different settings and contexts (e.g., community based program, school, case management, inpatient psychiatric and residential programs) impact IST practice. There are several examples where IST supervision may not be a good fit. For instance, a training program that heavily trains their students to be psychoanalytic therapists and does not value systemic integration. Or a mental health agency only wants their interns and employees to practice Gottman Couple

Therapy Method, which occurred with the first author's therapist. There are circumstances where there are no particular requirements in the therapist's profession or work settings that prohibit IST supervision. That leaves room for negotiation and flexibility if the therapist is open to or passionate about seeking IST supervision.

Situations Involving Risk

One of the supervisor's main responsibilities is to help the therapist develop sensibility to recognize risk issues and the ability to handle crisis situations. The common risks in systemic therapy include the client's intention to hurt themselves or others, child abuse, elder abuse, domestic violence, and sexual abuse. Laws in all 50 states in the US require a therapist to contact authorities and/or others if the therapist suspects that a known child is being abused. The supervisor helps the therapist to carefully assess the potential risks and determine appropriate steps to protect clients' safety. Depending on the severity of the case and the competency of the therapist, the supervisor determines whether the therapist can deliver proper services to the client.

The IST's hypothesizing matrix (Figure 1.3) and the cost-effectiveness guideline prioritize more direct and less complicated intervention at the beginning of therapy. That is, the therapist begins using the sequences, organization, and development hypothesizing metaframeworks. The interpersonal guideline indicates that when possible and appropriate, it is always better to do an intervention, regardless of its nature, within an interpersonal as opposed to an individual context. When risk situations happen, those guidelines do not apply. As indicated by Russell et al. (2023), risk issues surpass all the principles and guidelines of IST including the alliance and should be the top priority of therapy. The supervisor must advise the therapist to properly assess the severity of the risk and take action that adheres to the best practice in their field.

In a relational therapy context, when the therapist suspects that any member may experience risks such as child abuse, domestic violence, and sexual abuse, the therapist should schedule individual sessions with the member of concern and gather more information to assess the situation appropriately. If the risks pose safety concerns for the family member, then the focus must be centered on protecting the family member's safety. There are several possible solution sequences to address the safety issue. The supervisor may urge the therapist to contact the outside community agencies such as the state department of child protection, the police department, or a local mental health facility (Russell et al., 2023). When this path is determined to be the best and necessary plan, the supervision is focused on teaching the therapist the protocol and procedures for safety planning. If it is determined by both the supervisor and the therapist that the risk is manageable, then another solution may be helping the client commit to a safety plan and constantly assessing the client's risk. In the couple and family therapy context, the supervisor may suggest the therapist switch the therapy context to individual.

Risk management is always a balance of helping the therapist learn a critical skill and protecting clients from harm. When clients' safety is at risk and deemed not an appropriate training case, the supervisor validates the challenges of working with high-risk issues and explains that the clients' care is beyond the therapist's current developmental stage and capability. The supervisor may suggest the therapist refer the clients to a more experienced therapist or agency that specializes in specific issues.

High-risk situations do not only happen in the client system. The supervisor pays attention to the well-being of the therapist and how it affects their competence at a given time. For therapists still in an academic program, they may be juggling school, internship, work, and personal life and family. For therapists who work in an agency postgraduation, they may have a heavy clinical caseload. For therapists who manage their own private practice, they take on administrative responsibilities such as billing. Therapists may experience negative life events and their stress level quickly jumps up. In light of the concerns and life challenges, the supervisor regularly checks in with the therapist about their life and incorporates the plan for self-care in supervision. If the supervisor notices a therapist is too exhausted to be present with a client, discussions about pausing clinical work should be brought up in supervision.

Changing Contexts of Therapy

IST redefines treatment modality (i.e., individual therapy, couple therapy, and family therapy) as *context of therapy* that involves the family/community, couple/co-parent, and individual context because the term "modality" is too rigid to capture the natural human systems (Pinsof et al., 2017; see Figure 1.3 in Chapter 1). There are some flexibilities of changing therapy contexts reflected by the double-direction arrows in Figure 1.3. It is crucial to make changes to the therapy contexts in a thoughtful manner—such changes can bring up ethical considerations. The supervisor helps the therapist make decisions about whether changing from one therapy context to another is ethical. It is generally acceptable to move from a larger therapy context (e.g., couple/co-parent) to smaller therapy context (e.g., individual) when the clients in the larger context agree and the therapist feels comfortable with this shift. If the therapist thinks that knowing the client from a previous context may lead to bias, it may be better to refer them to another therapist. In contrast, some clients want to change back to a relational context after shifting to a smaller context. Moving from a smaller context to a larger context is not recommended because it is difficult to maintain therapeutic alliance with all the people after the therapist closely works with some members in individual therapy.

Relational Ethics

Ethics do not only refer to the code of ethics in the mental health professions; they also exist in clients' lives. That is, just as the therapist needs to make ethical decisions in clinical work, clients also have to make ethical decisions in their lives. Psychotherapy is developed in western culture where there is a strong emphasis on individual interests and independence. People tend to prioritize their self-interests when facing an ethical dilemma in life, and this tendency is often validated and supported by psychotherapists. Therefore, psychotherapy runs a risk of only attending to an individual client's self-interests and ignoring the potential negative impact of the client's behaviors on others in their lives. A few articles and books have been devoted to the topic of relational ethics (e.g., Doherty, 2008, 2022; Wrape et al., 2019). They suggest a concept called "relational self" that individuals' relationships are an important aspect of their self-concept and the therapist must help the clients to have a balance of fulfilling their own interests while maintaining their sense of responsibility and commitments to others (e.g., a disabled parent, a traumatized child, a wounded spouse) and society.

The beliefs of relational ethics are consistent with IST. IST urges the therapist to have a systemic view of the therapeutic alliance which includes not only the alliance between the therapist in the direct client system but also the alliance between the therapist and people in the indirect client system. Thus, we believe the supervisor should increase the therapist's knowledge about relational ethics and promote their ability to conduct ethical consultation when a client brings up an ethical dilemma in session. For instance, a client feels overwhelmed with taking care of their elderly parents and wonders about whether they should abandon them to release their own stress. Hearing this, the therapist can no longer stay neutral because the client's behavior can lead to serious negative consequences for their parents who are significant persons in their life. If we truly believe the idea of "relational self", abandoning elderly parents may help to alleviate the client's stress temporarily, but the client may experience tremendous feelings of guilt later which negatively affect them in the long run. The client's parents, although not attending therapy, are important resources for the client's well-being. Different from usual therapy conversations, the therapist will go through the steps of listening and validating the client's feelings without showing agreement, affirming that they have ethical responsibilities as adult children, providing a perspective inviting the client to consider the impact on their parents and their relationships with them, and challenging the client when necessary. Doherty (2022) has detailed descriptions of the rationale and procedures of conducting ethical consultation. The supervisor can attend relevant trainings (see https://relationalethic sintherapy.org) so that they can teach their therapists the skills of ethical consultation when it is appropriate.

Evaluation of IST Supervision Outcomes

How does the supervisor evaluate supervision outcomes? There are a multitude of ways a supervisor can evaluate a therapist's development. For instance, the supervisor can generate an assessment plan and collaborate with the therapist to execute it. The supervisor can provide verbal feedback or use quantitative measures to provide written feedback. The supervisor can develop specific items that assess the therapist's ability to utilize the IST tools such as the essence, blueprint, and guidelines. For example, the supervisor can rate on a Likert scale from 1 to 5 how well the therapist performs each of the IST essence tasks with the goal of effective and ethical client care. The ratings should be based on the therapist's developmental stage. The supervisor can evaluate the skills based on case consultation over time (e.g., six months), a videotaped case, or a live supervision case. In the MSMFT program at The Family Institute at Northwestern University, there is a capstone requirement that asks students to submit video clips of them performing the IST essence operations. Each student's video clip segments are evaluated by the faculty and supervisor to assess their competence. Additional assessments can be developed to assess the blueprint operation, such as the therapist's conversational skills and alliance maintenance skills which are described more in Chapter 6. Lastly, the supervisory alliance can also be measured and discussed on a regular basis.

The supervisor needs to decide a timeline that lists the frequency of evaluation, small goals during each short period of time, evaluations forms, and evaluators. The therapist's goals and their development are also included in the evaluation. For instance, if the therapist wants to develop specialty in certain interventions, their competence in this area can be evaluated as well. The therapist's overall development attends to their use of self effectively, their ability to build therapeutic alliance, and their acquisition of risk management skills for handling safety and crisis situations. Those aspects need to be evaluated regularly by the supervisor. The evaluator may also involve the supervisor, the therapist themselves, and peers if in group supervision. When the evaluations are done, the supervisor follows up with the therapist to provide verbal and written feedback based on the results. The supervisor can also track the progress according to the evaluations conducted at different times. The evaluations should be conducted in a formal way, and the therapist can clearly see their improvement and how much they have accomplished. The supervisor provides compliments and encouragement, expresses concerns if there are any, and discusses a future plan for the therapist to continue improving their competency and development.

References

Doherty, W. J. (2008). *Soul searching: Why psychotherapy must promote moral responsibility*. Basic Books.

Doherty, W. J. (2022). *The ethical lives of clients: Transcending self-interest in psychotherapy*. American Psychological Association.

Mosley, M. A., Parker, M. L., & Call, T. (2022). MFT supervision in the era of telehealth: Attachment, tasks, and ethical considerations. *Journal of Family Therapy*, 44(2), 224–238. https://doi.org/10.1111/1467-6427.12352.

Pinsof, W. M., Breunlin, D. C., Russell, W. P., Lebow, J. L., Rampage, C., & Chambers, A. L. (2017). *Integrative systemic therapy: Metaframeworks for problem solving with individuals, couples, and families*. American Psychological Association.

Russell, W. P., Breunlin, D. C., & Sahebi, B. (2023). *Integrative systemic therapy in practice: A clinician's handbook*. Routledge.

Wootton, A. R., McCuistian, C., Legnitto Packard, D. A., Gruber, V. A., & Saberi, P. (2020). Overcoming technological challenges: Lessons learned from a telehealth counseling study. *Telemedicine and e-Health*, 26(10), 1278–1283. https://doi.org/10.1089/tmj.2019.0191.

Wrape, E. R., & McGinn, M. M. (2019). Clinical and ethical considerations for delivering couple and family therapy via telehealth. *Journal of Marital and Family Therapy*, 45(2), 296–308. https://doi.org/10.1111/jmft.12319.

Chapter 5

The Development of the Integrative Systemic Supervisor

Becoming an IST supervisor is a considerable task. The journey is easier for some people in some aspects and harder for others in different areas, depending on their past clinical training and clinical experiences. Once the supervisor fully adopts IST as their supervision meta-perspective, they are guaranteed to have a solid foundation on which to add new knowledge and skills. This chapter is written for supervisors who are curious about how to develop oneself to be an IST supervisor. It begins with describing the uniqueness of the supervisor's developmental trajectory, transitions to list different elements of the supervisor's competence, pathways, and development stages, discusses self-of-the-supervisor issues, and ends with the impact of training background on supervisor development.

The Overall Developmental Trajectory of an IST Supervisor

One common question for the supervisor is whether they need to primarily use IST in their clinical practice to supervise others using the IST framework. With most supervision approaches, it is common that the supervisor is trained in a specific therapy model as a therapist and then they grow into the role of a supervisor in that model. For instance, a solution-focused therapist receives extensive training in solution-focused therapy, and they later become a supervisor guiding therapists practicing this therapy model. Some therapy models have designated pathways for a therapist to gain certification in their methods which usually involves receiving a certain amount of supervision from certified supervisors/trainers in that approach. In this case, the trajectory from being a therapist to being a supervisor is concentrated on developing competence in the specific theory and method.

The developmental trajectory of an IST supervisor may be different from this path. An IST supervisor does not necessarily have a history of IST being central in their own training and may practice any specific schools of therapy. What is essential is that supervisors are familiar with the essential tools of IST and know how to implement them effectively. We consider it as one of the strengths of the IST approach to supervision because it provides

DOI: 10.4324/9781003146841-5

flexibility and accommodates various developmental stages/pathways of the supervisor. Similar to therapist development, the supervisor does not abandon the expertise they have developed in certain models while providing IST supervision. The supervisor can utilize IST as the supervision framework and at the same time they practice from particular models in their clinical work. They benefit from keeping the commitment to their "home" approach when working with clients and shaping their therapist's competence and development through the IST lens. For example, the supervisor may emphasize the principles and methods of cognitive behavioral couple therapy (Baucom et al., 2015) and the therapist may primarily work in the context of principles and methods of emotionally focused couple therapy (EFT, Johnson, 2012). Utilizing the IST approach to supervision allows this training experience to transcend these models and provides a common language. The supervisor who fully practices in an IST framework or another integrative approach would also find the IST supervision framework easy to adapt.

Supervisor Competence

In general, the supervisor needs to have general knowledge of the skills required for clinical supervision in one's profession (e.g., American Psychological Association, 2014; American Association for Marriage and Family Therapy, 2014), such as establishing goals and expectations, providing constructive feedback, helping therapists think about their cases in relational ways, and ensuring therapists adhere to the ethical guideline of their profession and national/local laws and regulations. Moreover, supervisors can build and maintain a supervisory alliance with therapists. This alliance includes a professional relationship of "trust, openness, vulnerability, and commitment to quality training" (Lee & Nelson, 2014, p. 10). Supervisors also strive for multicultural humility, and have education and training in feedback and evaluation, legal and ethical standards, gatekeeping, and developmental tasks that arise in supervision (Bernard & Goodyear, 2014). In addition, the supervisor should have received systemic therapy training and have the ability to work across therapy contexts (i.e., family, couple, individual).

Those general competencies can be pursued by attending supervisor training, seeking peer consultation, reading about supervision, accumulating supervision experiences under mentorship (also called supervision of supervision). For example, the American Association for Marriage and Family Therapy (AAMFT) has the approved supervisor designation which involves a 30-hour fundamentals of supervision course and a minimum of 180 hours of supervising MFTs or MFT trainees under the supervision of an Approved Supervisor mentor (AAMFT, 2014). Many counseling, clinical psychology, and MFT doctoral programs offer courses in how to provide adequate supervision. On the American Psychological Association website, they offer various supervision workshops. There are webinars within professional organizations or private companies that are tailored to specific supervision topics, such as navigating supervision during COVID-19 and providing tele-supervision. It is best for the first-time supervisor to have a supervision mentor who they can lean on for support, feedback, and encouragement. And the supervisor wants to always assess their alliance with the therapists, the alliance between therapists if group supervision, and the alliance between the supervisor and the therapists as a group.

Before we summarize the specific competencies relevant to IST super-vision, we would review what the IST therapist's competencies entail. The competencies of the IST therapist are described in both Chapter 6 and He et al. (2023) in detail, which are briefly summarized here. First, the IST thera-pist recognizes IST's theoretical pillars and applies them in clinical work. Second, the IST therapist uses the IST essence diagram and blueprint effec-tively to maintain good therapeutic alliance with clients and generate desir-able treatment outcomes. The IST therapist also utilizes the seven hypothesizing metaframeworks and planning metaframeworks to guide their choices of interventions when implementing solution sequences and remov-ing constraints. Overall, the therapist follows the 11 IST guidelines and incorporates empirical evidence in their treatment planning and interven-tions. The therapist also learns how to use themselves effectively for posi-tively contributing to the therapy processes and outcomes. Finally, beyond the skill acquisition of IST tools and their clinical application, the therapist establishes a professional identity as an integrative systemic therapist through self-reflections, supervision and mentoring, and accumulation of clinical experiences. In this section, we discuss how to master the IST fra-mework through readings and training and use IST to track supervision dynamics and problem-solve issues happening in supervision.

Mastering the IST Framework

Consistent with the above competencies that the IST therapist needs to establish, there are some unique competencies required of the IST super-visor. They have a general understanding of the transtheoretical perspective, systemic theory, and integrative approach that IST offers. Therapists typi-cally will also be curious about the supervisor's own practice—especially regarding the use of IST. The supervisor has a clear grasp of the theoretical pillars, essence of IST, and blueprint as well as the guidelines and how they look in case conceptualization and the therapist's interactions with clients.

The way that the IST supervisor learns about IST and family systems theory training is similar to the learning process of the therapist explained in Chapter 3. This begins with being knowledgeable about the IST frame-work. The supervisor can read the two IST books (Pinsof et al., 2018; Rus-sell et al., 2023) and a few IST journal articles and book chapters (e.g., Breunlin et al., 2011; Chambers, 2019; Hardy et al., 2019; He et al., 2021,

2022; Pinsof et al., 2011; Russell & Breunlin, 2019; Russell et al., 2016). Only mastering the IST framework is not enough for the supervisor to provide comprehensive guidance to promote the therapist's growth. The supervisor must be capable of conceptualizing cases through the IST lens and implementing a variety of clinical interventions and techniques that fall into the planning metaframeworks in the IST matrix. Those skills are essential for training the IST therapist as the supervisor expects the therapist to do the same thing. With that being said, the supervisor may obtain additional training depending on their current knowledge and clinical experiences.

According to IST's ontological pillar, having a deep understanding of systems theory and related concepts is a prerequisite to providing IST supervision. If the supervisor cannot orient themselves to operationalize the basic concepts such as cybernetics, recursiveness, isomorphism, homeostasis, feedback loops, and equifinality, it would be impossible for them to either help the therapist appropriately use IST or use IST to guide the supervision process. Therefore, it is important for supervisors with an individual-focused training background to receive extra training in this area. The supervisor may attend workshops and webinars, take classes, and receive mentorship from systemic supervisors to achieve the goal of conceptualizing and intervening cases at both interpsychic and intrapsychic levels. The supervisor may find systemic training resources on the AAMFT website (www.aamft.org). Some organizations provide systemic therapy training. For example, the Ackerman Institute for the Family in New York provides a 30-week introductory course that prepares mental health professionals for advanced training in systemic therapy which can be delivered in person or online. The Family Institute at Northwestern University offers postgraduate fellowship and postdoctoral clinical scholar fellowship that train therapists to practice within a systemic lens. Another example is PESI, a not-profit organization offering continuing education including family therapy courses to mental health professions. If supervisors are interested in learning about specific family therapy approaches, they can pursue training in particular family therapy institutes and centers (e.g., the Minuchin Center for the Family, the Bowen Center for the Study of the Family, the Family Therapy Center of Milan).

IST embraces interventions from both systemic and individual-focused therapy approaches. It is helpful to seek training on individual-oriented therapy methods (e.g., cognitive behavioral therapy, psychoanalytic therapy, emotion-focused therapy) if the supervisor is trained only in the systemic therapy framework. The supervisor can visit professional organizations' websites depending on their clinical interests, such as the American Psychological Association, the American Counseling Association, the National Association of Cognitive-Behavioral Therapists, the International Society for Emotion Focused Therapy, the American Psychoanalytic Association, the International Psychoanalytic Association, and the Beck Institute.

The purpose is not to build expertise in those individual therapy theories although it can be the supervisor's personal goal. Instead, the purpose is to know how to implement some of the common intervention methods from the theories, such as identifying and changing the client's distorted beliefs, gaining insights about the impact of childhood experiences on their current problems, and processing unresolved emotions from the past. Then the supervisor can coach the therapist to draw individual-focused interventions from the planning metaframeworks.

There are different methods that the supervisor can use to facilitate the therapist's mastering of the IST framework. The supervisor can ask Socratic questions to help the therapist form their case conceptualization about specific cases following the IST essence and blueprint. The supervisor can provide education and lead discussion about certain topics (e.g., how to identify problem sequences, how to remove constraints) if the therapist needs to acquire specific IST skills. The supervisor can do role-plays for either case consultation or skills development. The supervisor can share their own cases and model how they use IST for their clinical work. Watching the therapist's session videos can provide the supervisor with great information about how the therapist applies the IST tools and concepts. The supervisor can identify where the therapist does a good job and where the therapist gets stuck or misses certain steps. Observing a live therapy session serves a similar purpose but also allows the supervisor to provide instant feedback while the therapist is working with the client system.

Using IST to Track Sequences and Problem-Solve in Supervision

Supervisors need expertise both in clinical work and in the practice of IST supervision—competence in the former is not enough for competence in the latter. As such, in addition to some level of proficiency in the practice of IST, competence as an IST supervisor needs to be developed. The IST supervisor understands the multi-level system of client–therapist–supervisor, and how these levels impact and relate to one another. IST supervision involves a core competency of using IST tools to track sequences and solve problems as they occur in the supervision context, and hypothesizing about the therapist's development (or culture, mind, etc.) relating to their areas of clinical competency and their own development.

Using the IST essence and blueprint, the supervisor observes the sequences that occur in the therapist system and the client system, which takes practice. Ideally, the therapist gains constructive feedback from their supervisor and peers (if group supervision) and translates the feedback into their own development of skills and personal styles, which is then reflected in their interactions with the client system. The supervisor observes how the conversations occurring in supervision impact the therapy room or vice versa. The supervisor offers insights to help the therapist make clinical decisions while honoring spaces for the therapist to explore their own thoughts and owing their session. For example, when a supervisor provides direction in supervision, does the therapist own this intervention with the client, or do they triangulate—intentionally or not—saying, "my supervisor told me to try out this strategy with you," thus bringing in a power dynamic in the room and potentially harming the therapy process? Such a client may feel cautious about questioning the intervention if it is coming from an "all wise" supervisor who is not in the room to be questioned. Furthermore, the supervisor needs to pay extra attention to group dynamics in group supervision. The supervisor makes sure that they maintain a good supervisory relationship with each of the therapists, have a balanced way to divide time in supervision, and create a group atmosphere that the members think is fair and supportive.

It is important for the supervisor to make sure that the same supervision goals are shared and all parties in supervision are open to discuss potential problems and constraints that they find throughout the process. The supervisor also role-models this open communication so that the therapist can do the same with their clients. Here we attempt to address several common problems and constraints in supervision using IST.

The therapist may experience difficulty implementing specific IST tools, such as identifying constraints or having effective communication with clients using the blueprint. The supervisor tries to understand the problem sequence around the difficulty, hypothesize the potential constraints, and explore solutions with the therapist. The problem sequence may be related to the following factors: Does the therapist have a good understanding of the tool? Does the supervisor provide proper guidance teaching and facilitating the learning of the tool? How does the therapist practice the tool in clinical work? How many times does the therapist try implementing it? What are the client system's responses? How does the supervisor help the therapist evaluate their implementation? How does the supervisor encourage the therapist to try it again or try something different?

A vignette was provided in Chapter 3 regarding how to identify and lift the therapist Sue's constraints of having little knowledge about the role of gender in family dynamics, which resulted in an unbalanced therapeutic alliance with family members. Here is another example. A therapist may have a cultural constraint regarding learning to work with clients who have sexual health concerns. In the therapist's culture, asking clients about sexual health may be seen as shameful or invasive. The IST supervisor would track how this potential discomfort or resistance may show up in a sequence during supervision as well as in therapy. The IST supervisor would work together with the therapist to remove the constraint.

Another common challenge is that the therapist is not receptive to the supervisor's feedback when the feedback is much needed to accomplish the client system's goal. The supervisor uses the IST blueprint to hypothesize about what prevents the therapist from being more open. The supervisor considers all the hypothesizing metaframeworks and identifies what may be the constraints. The supervisor first reflects what role they and other members of supervision play in this problem. The supervisor wonders whether their warmth and encouragement are not in place to allow the therapist to consider their feedback or bring up disagreement. The supervisor also thinks whether anything they or group members did in the past makes the therapist uncomfortable. The supervisor then examines whether the therapist's developmental stages, personality, cultural values, gender, perceptions of the supervision relationships, and personal biases can be the constraints. It is possible that the therapist believes that they are at a more advanced developmental stage than they really are, or they are much older than the supervisor. Therefore, they do not consider it necessary to incorporate the supervisor's advice. The therapist may have a hard time receiving feedback because they tend to feel offended when others show disagreement. The therapist may come from a different cultural background than the supervisor and thus does not easily trust the supervisor's judgment. The therapist may be a cisgender White male who has a hard time considering an ethnic minority female supervisor's suggestion. The therapist may not realize the hierarchical relationship that exists between the supervisor and the therapist, and therefore does not take the supervisor seriously. The therapist may be stuck with their own biases due to a lack of awareness of their limitations and blind spots. For example, a cisgender female therapist denies the supervisor's feedback about exploring the impact of societal stigma that their transgender clients may experience. Another example could be a White therapist rejects the supervisor's suggestions about examining racial trauma that their Black clients may experience. A highly educated therapist who grows up in a wealthy family may not be receptive to understanding the lack of financial resources among lower-middle-class clients.

Through self-reflection or the therapist's evaluation, the supervisor may realize that they have not successfully built a good supervisory alliance. The supervisor hypothesizes the potential problem sequence and constraints. Does the therapist agree with the goals and tasks in supervision? Does the supervisor connect with the therapist and provide enough support, which is one of the main common factors for supervision (Morgan & Sprenkle, 2007)? Does the supervisor play a good leadership role and set up appropriate rules for providing a stable and clear structure? Is the therapist compliant with the rules and policies? Similar to the definition of the systemic alliance in therapy, the supervisor also examines the alliance between the therapists if in group supervision, the alliance between the entire group of therapists and themselves, and the alliance between each therapist and themselves.

The supervisor tracks what happens before, during, and after the poor supervisory relationship, and then tries to come up with solution sequences. For example, a therapist may perceive the supervisor to be too critical and then shut down during supervision. The supervisor apologizes to the therapist and discusses ways of being more supportive of the therapist. The poor supervisory relationship can occur in group supervision. For instance, when one therapist is too dominant by taking too much time, other therapists get frustrated and withdraw from the conversations. The supervisor assumes their leadership role and lets everyone know that the time in supervision needs to be fairly shared among the therapists over time.

Cultural Similarities and Differences in Supervision

With the world becoming increasingly diverse, it is not uncommon that supervisors, therapists, and clients share different cultural backgrounds such as race/ethnicity, social class, gender identity, spirituality and religious affiliation, and sexual orientation. Such diversity enriches supervision experiences by adding various perspectives. It also creates challenges when misunderstanding and lack of cultural humility occurs. It can help the therapist if the supervisor shares their relevant experiences, especially if the supervisor shares a cultural context with the therapist. However, it can also create blind spots as the supervisor may over identify with the therapist and miss the differences between them due to the complexity of human intersectionality and heterogeneity existing within similar cultures and countries. Cultural differences can also create blind spots. IST supervision provides a framework to interact and conceptualize between the various micro and macro levels that exist between the supervisor, student, and the client's worlds.

Puja is an Asian female supervisor who immigrated from India. She works with Isabella who is an immigrant from Honduras. Isabella has difficulty saying no to her clients even when the client's request is not reasonable. She starts building resentment and feeling taken advantage of. When Puja helps Isabella figure out the source of her discomfort, Puja uses the IST blueprint to hypothesize that Isabella's past immigration status may play a role. After Puja shares her hypothesis, Isabella bursts into tears. She never makes the connection, but this hypothesis surprisingly makes sense to her. Isabelle indeed encounters many obstacles during the immigration process, which prompts her to dread being deported if she says no. Therefore, she is alert to others' needs and feels strongly to prioritize them. Puja validates Isabelle's concerns and briefly shares her immigration experiences. Puja made it clear that her experiences may be different from Isabella's in many ways. Puja also helps Isabelle to understand that she no longer needs to be so cautious working with clients, and she has every right to have her needs too in therapy. Through hypothesizing, planning, conversing, and receiving feedback, Puja discloses her own immigration experiences to connect with Isabelle and support her to express her needs. This example echoes a social justice perspective valued in IST supervision.

Three Paths of the Supervisor

IST supervisors tend to experience some variation of the following three paths: (1) supervisors who are trained in IST as therapists and are developing IST supervision competency; (2) supervisors who are established more in other specific approaches, and are looking for a unifying meta-perspective from which to supervise the variety of approaches used by therapists they supervise; or (3) supervisors who may not know IST very well but end up working or training in a setting in which IST is the therapy and supervision framework. Each of these paths involves developing specific competencies in supervision more generally (Path 1) or learning IST and how it looks in clinical practice and supervision (Paths 2 and 3).

The process of learning to effectively implement the tools of IST as a supervisor may have both advantages and challenges when they are on different paths. Path 1 seems straightforward while the supervisor needs more training on being a competent supervisor in general. They can seek out supervisor training in their academic programs, agencies, and professional organizations which may involve mentorship from a more experienced supervisor. The supervisors on Paths 2 and 3 have expertise in specific therapy models and may have been practicing for years in these approaches. Naturally, they tend to think about their therapist's cases through these lenses. What they need is to incorporate the IST paradigm into psychotherapy practice and supervision, which need not mean replacing their previously favored methods. Given that IST supervision requires stepping outside of the comfort zone of one or two home theories, the stretch involved in considering a broader palette of interventions may be a constraint to supervisor development. For example, a supervisor may find the idea of transtheoretical integration in supervision to be appealing, but they may become overwhelmed when they consider the numerous options that can potentially exist in the hypothesizing and planning metaframeworks. Or a supervisor might be excited to learn a few new interventions from other theories to help the therapist develop skills, but may have difficulty finding time to learn new ways of conceptualizing from other perspectives.

Supervision might also occur in the context of academic programs or agency settings in which there is a narrow focus on one theory and method of practice. In some settings, the therapist may be given the choice of which model to choose, but is instructed to choose a specific model, nonetheless. Other settings may support learning several models but lack a framework to organize the tools offered within each model. The supervisor may attempt to express their concerns about the therapist selecting one approach. They can try to persuade the stakeholders in the program or agency about reconsidering those rules. When the rules are ambiguous, there may be more room for communication and negotiation. The supervisor can negotiate at least minimally that the setting would allow them to provide IST supervision with no negative consequences. If not successful, the supervisor would have to accept it because their environment does not support IST learning and supervision.

Finally, an additional challenge can occur in IST supervision when the supervisor may be open to a variety of perspectives, but the therapist strongly gravitates to specializing in one specific model at the expense of additional ways of conceptualization and intervention. This can lead to tension as the supervisor encourages a more transtheoretical approach to assessment and intervention. The supervisor is suggested to not strongly push their own agenda on IST training and supervision because it can cause more resistance from the therapist. Like the vignette in Chapter 2, the supervisor can explore the therapist's goals and gently introduce IST and its benefits. Then the supervisor shows interest in the therapist's chosen approach and tries to make a connection between IST and their selected approach. For example, a therapist may be committed to learning and practicing emotionally focused therapy with their individuals, couples, and families. Although EFT-specific supervision may be available from other supervisors, the IST supervisor would work with this therapist first in identifying sequences from an EFT lens (e.g., pursue–withdraw sequences) and hypothesizing using attachment theory (e.g., unmet needs and under-lying fears drive the problem sequences). In this way, the IST supervisor meets the therapist where they are at, while introducing the IST framework which will allow the therapist to begin to add in conceptualizations and interventions from other models, when needed.

Developmental Stages for Supervisors Who Know about IST

Development as an IST supervisor may vary depending on one's clinical background and supervision experiences. The developmental stages for supervisors who are already trained in IST (Path 1) may be similar to the development of any individual learning to be a supervisor. In the first stage, the supervisor transitions from an IST therapist to the role of an IST supervisor. They are learning about the basic settings of IST supervision, such as developing one's own supervision contract and identifying the rules and policy of supervision. In the second stage, the supervisor has a deeper understanding of the complex dynamics between the supervision and therapy contexts as well as the advantages and limitations of having power. They are adjusting to a new role of authority who serves as a gatekeeper to prevent harm from happening to the client system. Their tolerance of uncertainty that occurs in supervision and therapy increases. They consider supervision as an independent professional activity. They are learning about the therapist's goals and styles, and avoiding imposing their own therapy styles on the therapist. The last stage is featured by a high awareness of their own supervision style and its advantages and limitations as well as a prolonged interest in supervision. They have confidence in their role as an IST supervisor and see this role as an important aspect of their professional identity.

A well-experienced IST therapist, Helena, is learning how to supervise a postgraduate therapist, Weiping. While Helena can teach IST concepts in supervision proficiently, she lacks training and experience as a supervisor. She makes common mistakes as a beginner supervisor, such as expecting Weiping to do therapy just the same way that she does. For example, she requires Weiping to converse with clients as directly as she might and to complete assessment of the problem sequences as soon as she can. Because Weiping is still trying to establish confidence in practicing IST, she finds Helena's expectations too high. Weiping feels discouraged and loses confidence. In this case, Helena may be a fantastic IST therapist. However, she ignores many predictors of successful supervision, including building supervisory alliance, providing encouragement, and considering the therapist's developmental level when assessing the therapist's competence. She should seek additional training, mentoring, and consultation opportunities to be a qualified systemic supervisor.

Developmental Stages for Supervisors Who Are New to IST

There are three common developmental stages applied to supervisors on Paths 2 and 3 who are unfamiliar with IST in their past training and begin to adopt IST in their supervision.

Stage 1: Learning about IST and Utilizing IST Language in Supervision

The supervisor begins learning about IST through readings and workshops and how to use it to guide the supervision process. Although they have not fully grasped all the concepts and their clinical application, the supervisor is eagerly beginning to incorporate IST in supervision. They may refer to IST terms here and there. For example, they may ask "What prevents the client system from implementing the solution sequence?" without helping the therapist understand the meaning of the problem sequence and solution sequence defined in IST. This supervisor may occasionally refer to the IST matrix as they work with their therapist. For instance, the supervisor asks the therapist how they choose the order of interventions based on the IST matrix. However, there is little comprehensive understanding of the process and presenting concerns, which are typically not looked at in terms of problem sequences. For example, the supervisor may ask the therapist about a variety of metaframeworks related to the problem, but neglect to locate the problem in a sequence. Figure 5.1 depicts the random and scattered selection and utilization of IST language in supervision without considering the theoretical pillars and particular IST tools.

Solution Sequence

Problem Sequence   Hypothesizing

Planning Matrix
                            Constraints
Planning

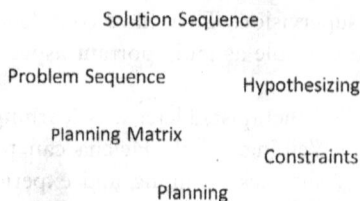

Figure 5.1 Utilizing IST Language in Supervision with No Use of the IST Theory

This developmental stage is very normal for beginning IST learners and supervisors. It can be compared to therapists who begin to learn a new theory. The supervisor may question their ability to conduct IST supervision appropriately. What they would typically do is to use the languages of that theory which gives them confidence that they are applying the theory. For example, a therapist who learns about solution-focused brief therapy (De Shazer et al., 2021) would use the miracle question and the scaling questions although they do not understand the theoretical assumptions of the therapy model or do not ask the questions in the right way. Just as the therapist needs to gain confidence in applying a therapy model, the supervisor also has the need to feel competent as an IST supervisor, which is normal and understandable.

Lindsey is a supervisor who comes to IST with little experience with its concepts. Her therapist, Aiden, is unfamiliar with IST and asks a lot of sophisticated questions about how to practice IST. Lindsey feels uneasy when she does not know the answers. Aiden notices Lindsey's lack of confidence which reduces his trust in Lindsey's supervisory competence. Their supervision is unproductive and tense, leaving both feeling frustrated and unsatisfied. In this scenario, the supervisor is at the initial developmental stage of implementing IST supervision. She needs to be transparent with the therapist about her expertise rather than pretending she "knows it all." She might draw on her strengths and competencies in other areas (e.g., ethics, systemic thinking, common factors) to help establish a stable positive supervisory alliance with the therapist.

Stage 2: Conducting IST supervision within the scope of limited therapy theories

At this stage, a supervisor may begin utilizing the essence of IST to help therapists identify the problem sequence, potential solution sequences, and constraints. In terms of interventions, the focus is limited to strategies from one or two specific models. This stage of IST supervision utilizes more IST concepts and even uses IST as their overarching framework in supervision but still primarily focuses on conceptualization and intervention from the therapist's or supervisor's core approaches. For example, in Figure 5.2, a supervisor who typically utilizes emotionally focused therapy and internal

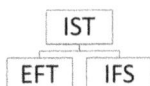

Figure 5.2 Example of Supervisor at Stage 2

family systems may use the essence diagram in supervision to track the problem sequence and identify the solution sequence. However, their conceptualization of the problem sequence and solution sequence stay within the concepts and interventions of these two theories. They tend to only draw intervention and strategies from these two approaches when they consider the IST matrix. Guiding the therapist's clinical work, the supervisor may conceptualize the problem sequence to be the conflict between parts within each person's mind, and the solution sequence is to heal these wounded parts and harmonize the relationships between all the parts. In addition, they only use IST for guiding the therapist's case consultation. They have not yet applied IST to view the sequence that occurs in supervision (e.g., between therapists, between the supervisor and the therapist, between supervision and its contexts, and within therapists). In this case, although the key concepts from the essence of IST are utilized, they are viewed through a limited perspective of one or two theories and only applied in the therapy context.

Stage 3: Transtheoretical Integration

At this stage, the IST supervisor can transcend specific models in their own clinical work and in supervision. Transtheoretical integration—as opposed to eclecticism or assimilative integration—is now the guiding principle of supervision (see Figure 5.3). They would begin case consultation using IST, go to specific therapy models to draw useful

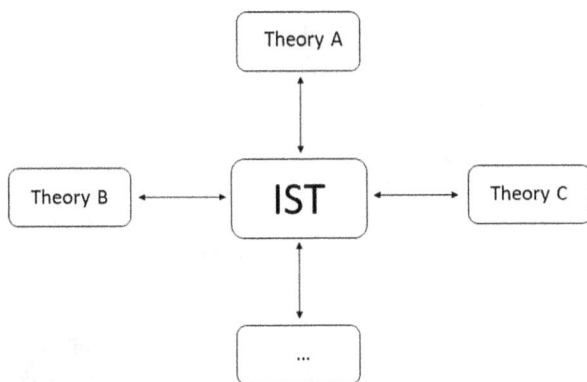

Figure 5.3 Conceptualization of Using IST for Transtheoretical Integration

concepts and interventions, and come back to IST framework for evaluating whether the interventions can contribute to the solution sequence or remove a constraint using the essence and blueprint. The supervisor does not only utilize IST as a supervision framework; the supervisor also explores and learns more about how to use techniques from a variety of models. This may be accomplished through additional clinical training, readings, peer consultation, and mentoring activities. Interventions from a variety of approaches are suggested as the supervisor and therapist look for ways to lift constraints to the problem sequences. Hypothesizing, planning, and conversing may be drawn from potentially any established treatment approach and research. More importantly, the supervisor views the therapist system including supervision through the IST lens. They are comfortable to use IST tools to address any sequence in the therapist system.

Michael, a supervisor who used to provide supervision based on his expertise in cognitive behavioral therapy, now can conceptualize cases within the IST framework and utilize interventions from other therapy approaches in his own practice and supervision. His change begins with attending a workshop on IST supervision and realizing the limitations of supervising therapists only through CBT. While learning about IST, he becomes more open to learning about other therapy approaches. Thus, he participates in clinical training on emotion-focused therapy and narrative therapy, enabling him to see the overlap and the differences of these approaches via the concepts of sequences and constraints. Furthermore, Michael expands his use of IST to address any issues that come up in the therapist/supervisor system and promote the therapist's development.

The IST supervisor does not progress through developmental stages in a linear way. Given that IST asks supervisors to draw upon a wide range of interventions, beginning supervisors may experience a steep learning curve as they expand their breadth of clinical knowledge. Experienced supervisors who practice in an integrative way often find it easier to quickly adopt IST supervision given their experiences in therapy and supervision and familiarity with a variety of treatment approaches. Even when the supervisor transitions from one stage to the next, micro-transitions such as learning how to guide therapists applying a new IST concept and its application may be necessary. The supervisor may move back and forth between stages, which corresponds with the concept of oscillation that the new competency co-exists with the lesser competency at a former stage (Breunlin, 1988). Transitions may take only months or up to a number of years to achieve. They require the supervisor to consistently self-reflect, seek supervision of supervision, and make efforts to absorb new knowledge from IST and the ever-evolving field of clinical practice and supervision.

Self-of-the-Supervisor

The Supervisor's Use of Self

In the psychotherapy literature, the topic of the self-of-the-therapist (also known as person-of-the-therapist) has been widely discussed (e.g., Aponte et al., 2009, 2016; Regas et al., 2017; Timm & Blow, 1999). The self-of-the-therapist work is defined as "the willingness of a therapist or supervisor to participate in a process that requires introspective work on issues in his or her own life, that has an impact on the process of therapy in both positive and negative ways" (Timm & Blow, 1999, p. 333). Because of the multi-systemic nature of IST supervision described in Chapter 2, the supervisor constantly interacts with the therapist directly and the client system indirectly. Like the therapist whose personal experiences would impact their clinical work, the supervisor brings their worldviews, life experiences, and social contexts to supervision. Those influences can be resources or constraints. Essentially, supervisors need to be attuned to how their patterns impact the developmental trajectory of the therapist as well as their more immediate work with their clients. Seeing that role and working on altering any dynamics seems like an important first step, and, if needed, to go deeper into the IST matrix of identifying personal or past issues that could explain how these patterns are emerging and taking hold, and then working to resolve those.

One important task for the supervisor is to promote their therapist's self-care. Similarly, the supervisor also needs to attend to their own well-being and mental health by involving in diverse activities, such as eating enough, enjoying different kinds of movement, getting enough sleep, having a balanced workload, or engaging in personal therapy. In addition to personal therapy, there are other ways to reduce stress and enrich one's self-reflection and learning, including retreats, continuing education, support groups, meditation, and other ways of enhancement available locally and on the internet.

The Supervisor's Experiences

Aspects of the supervisor's experiences are consistent with IST's web of human experiences, including organization, development, culture, mind, gender, biology, and spirituality. Organization here refers to the supervisor's ability to play a leadership role, set boundaries (e.g., set up ground rules), manage resources to meet the therapist's needs, and maintain a harmonious supervisory relationship. Development demonstrates the supervisor's capacity to attend to their own and their therapist's developmental stage and its corresponding tasks. Culture involves the supervisor's awareness of the dynamics between the cultural backgrounds of their own, the therapist, and the client. For example, which dimensions of their cultural contexts (i.e., membership) are the same or different? How do those similarities and differences impact supervision and therapy? Furthermore, the supervisor needs to understand how their mind functions and its effect on the supervisor's development. The supervisor also recognizes the interrelationships between their gender identity/gender roles and the gender identity and gender roles of the therapist and the client. Last but not least, the supervisor should pay attention to the biology and spirituality of their own, the therapist, and the client. For instance, when the supervisor feels burned out and begins developing physical symptoms (e.g., muscle tension and headache), what do they do to take care of themselves? If the supervisor is a Christian and would like to integrate doctrine and religious practices such as prayers in supervision, is it a good match with the therapist's needs?

Using IST to Develop the Supervisor's Self

In addition to using the web of human experiences, other tools of IST can be applied in helping the supervisor use oneself effectively. The supervisor can use the IST essence and blueprint to identify their strengths and growing areas. Particularly, the supervisor may draw ideas from the planning meta-frameworks (action, meaning/emotion, biobehavioral, family-of-origin, internal representation, and self) in the matrix (see Figure 1.3 in Chapter 1) when dealing with the negative impact of their internal patterns on supervision. Two vignettes are presented below.

Vignette: Self-Care

The supervisor, Astrid, in her late 30s, is a therapist and supervisor at a LGBTQ-affirmative mental health organization. She is a White cisgender lesbian, married and a mother of two young children, a five-year-old boy and a three-year-old girl. Her parents and younger sister, Ingrid, live nearby. Her partner, Katy, who works as a financial advisor, is supportive. Astrid is busy with fulfilling the responsibilities at work and at home. Her only sister, Ingrid, who is 30 years old, is recently diagnosed as having lung cancer. Astrid has a close relationship with Ingrid. She and her parents are devastated to learn about Ingrid's illness. Astrid visits Ingrid frequently and goes to doctor's appointments with her sometimes. She realizes that she could not fully concentrate on work, including supervision, because her mind is constantly worrying about Ingrid and anxious to know her treatment progress. In supervision, she finds herself getting triggered when the therapists' cases involve loss. She realizes that her personal worries become a constraint to her presence in supervision. After self-reflection, she recognizes that she has a pattern of putting too many responsibilities on herself and not asking for help, which is exacerbated within a cultural context that emphasizes individualism and independence. As a lesbian, she wants to perform well at work to minimize others' judgment. She realizes that she needs more social support and self-care during this difficult time. Astrid shares her concern about her mental health with Katy. Katy is very understanding and willing to take on more household/childcare responsibilities. For self-care, Astrid began engaging in mindfulness practices and yoga regularly, which helped her in the past. She also resumes therapy. She decides to not disclose her struggle to the therapists she supervises to keep the professional boundary. In supervision, she keeps reminding herself to breathe and gently bring herself back to the current moment when her mind wanders. She let her boss know about her sister's illness and receives support from her. Those efforts really help her to ground herself and deliver supervision effectively.

Vignette: Cultivating Cultural Awareness

The supervisor, Nicholas, is a White, heterosexual, cisgender man in his 50s who grows up in an affluent suburb in Connecticut. He moved to San Francisco in his 50s where he started his own private practice. In his therapy practice or supervision, he rarely brings up the topics of race, ethnicity, gender, sexual orientation, and social class. When his clients and therapists identify themselves as LGBTQ+ or Asian/Latino, he seldom explores how their cultural background contributes to the problem/solution sequence or constraints in therapy or supervision. He is also unaware of his privileges and how they impact his role as a therapist and a supervisor. He receives negative feedback particularly from his therapists and clients with minority backgrounds. They have a hard time trusting that Nicholas can relate to their experiences. There are occasions when his clients request to change to a different therapist. Luckily, he is an open-minded person. He finally realizes that he has work to do to resolve the problem of a lack of cultural awareness. However, he does not know where to start.

Nicholas goes to seek consultation from a senior therapist and supervisor, Alma, who is Latina and has expertise in multicultural practices and supervision. In his supervision of supervision, he reflects on how the problem is developed. It is mostly related to his family of origin and the small community where everyone shares similar values. He has limited knowledge and life experiences with people outside of his racial/ethnic identity, sexual orientation, and socioeconomic status. The clinical training that he received back in graduate school did not incorporate any multicultural components. The majority of his former clients and therapists in Connecticut share similar demographics. Nicholas wants to expand his view on the sequences, constraints, and strengths in therapy and supervision. After helping Nicholas realize the sequences that contribute to his lack of cultural awareness, Alma recommends him to attend a series of multiculturalism workshops where the facilitators provide a safe place for attendees to support each other going through a process of self-exploration and self-interrogation. In the beginning, Nicholas does not feel comfortable sharing vulnerabilities. Many participants are young therapists. He feels ashamed to be an experienced therapist and supervisor who acts like a beginner on this topic. He shares that with Alma. Alma challenges his distorted belief that experienced therapists should know about everything. Alma encourages him to take small steps to disclose his vulnerabilities. Nicholas agrees with her suggestion. He gradually shares more in the group. When he learns more about the vocabulary to discuss this difficult topic, he takes the courage to share how little he knows in the group and show how much he is willing to learn from others. The more he opens up, the more he realizes his limitations and how his therapy and supervision are impacted by them. Attending this workshop helps Nicholas tremendously. This is the beginning of hard work. He continues readings and supervision of supervision. He challenges himself to bring difficult topics in his own supervision with therapists and apologizes for his ignorance. He encourages his therapists to provide constructive feedback as he is still adjusting to a humbler and not-knowing position. He knows that it will take a lot of practice for him to embrace the idea of cultural humility in therapy and supervision.

Using IST to Address the Interaction of Supervisor and Therapist Development

The IST supervisor's self-development co-occurs with the therapist's development of becoming an IST therapist. How do these two forces interact with each other? How does such interaction impact the supervisory relationship and its effectiveness? The important tasks involve tracking the sequence between the supervisor and the therapist, recognizing the constraints that block the supervisor's ability to guide the therapist, and finding ways to remove the constraints. The supervisor needs to be self-reflective about their cognitions, emotions, and behaviors, and how they relate to the therapist's cognitions, feelings, and behaviors. The supervisor can use the blueprint to hypothesize, plan, converse, and seek feedback. Two vignettes are provided to demonstrate such interactions.

Vignette: Isomorphism among Supervisor–Therapist–Client Interactions

Louis is a supervisor candidate in his late 20s. He is a White, heterosexual, cisgender, middle-class man who is finishing his doctoral program. He is taking a supervision of supervision class in his program and receiving mentorship from his instructor, Diego, about providing supervision to a young African American master's student, Nia, who is in her second year and has started seeing clients at a local agency. Although he has extensive clinical experience, he is still adapting to this new role of supervisor. In their individual supervision, Louis notices that Nia tends to ask him what to do with her clients, which is common among new therapists in training.

Interestingly, Nia's clients expect her to provide a solution to their problems in therapy as well. Louis realizes there is an isomorphism between his interaction with Nia and Nia's interaction with her clients. The dynamic between therapy and supervision is similar. Louis and Nia both feel compelled to provide a straightforward answer when being asked. Otherwise, they feel anxious for not meeting the therapist/client's expectations and therefore believe that they are incompetent in their role as supervisor/therapist. According to IST's web of constraints, part of the reason is their developmental stage—Louis is a supervisor candidate and Nia is a new therapist in training. Gender and culture affect the interactive patterns in supervision and therapy as well.

Louis's supervision mentor, Diego, asks Louis what he is thinking and feeling when getting the question "what to do" from Nia. Louis reflects that he feels nervous and is afraid that Nia would perceive him as incompetent. In fact, Nia shows disappointment when she does not receive a direct answer from Louis (so do her clients!). When Diego helps Louis process his fear and sense of inadequacy, Louis reflects that he is generally concerned about disappointing others as his parents had high expectations of him growing up. He overcomes his fear while working with clients, but this issue resurfaces as he is adjusting to the role of a supervisor—which he perceives to have more power and authority than a therapist. He acknowledges that his privilege as a White, heterosexual male strengthens his belief that he needs to take an authoritative role. He often experiences tension in his neck and shoulders, and an increased heart rate in supervision.

Diego shares the hypothesis that Louis's early experiences and his view of his professional role constrain him from processing Nia's self-of-the therapist development in a candid way. Diego suggests Louis rethink his role in supervision. Does he consider himself as an experienced therapist who is supervising Nia to do therapy just as he would do it? If so, Louis needs to change his position to a trainer, mentor, or evaluator who pays more attention to the therapy and supervision process and dynamics. He should consider how to help Diego shape his own therapy style. Diego also challenges Louis to have an open discussion with Nia about how their racial backgrounds impact their relationship. Louis agreed with these suggestions.

In the next supervision meeting, Louis brings this pattern to Nia's attention. Although Louis does not disclose his childhood experience, he shares that he feels the pressure to address Nia's questions and protect her from feeling frustrated with his clients' disappointment. Then Louis tells Nia that he will not provide direct suggestions every time because it hinders Nia's own development as a therapist and thinking on her own. Nia quickly understands the rationale for Louis not giving her direct suggestions. She reflects on her anxiety of being a young therapist and feeling a lack of competence to help others. She also gains the insight that she is particularly worried about establishing competency when working with White male clients. When asked how their racial differences impact their supervision dynamics, Nia says that she initially feels intimidated working with a White supervisor, but Louis's humbleness and patience help her to build trust. In this supervision vignette, with the help of Diego, Louis reflected the impact of his early experiences and developmental stage on his supervisory relationship and effectiveness. This kind of isomorphism between supervision and therapy is common.

Vignette: Providing IST Supervision to Therapists Focusing on a Specific Therapy Approach

In IST supervision, a unique self-of-the-supervisor topic may emerge: The supervisor is very enthusiastic about the transtheoretical approach of IST while the therapist is strongly aligned with one specific model. Valencia, a Latina female supervisor in her mid-40s, provides supervision to Humphrey, a White male therapist in training in his 50s. Valencia is strongly committed to being an IST therapist as well as an IST supervisor. Humphrey is interested in IST, and he is also highly attracted to emotionally focused couple therapy (EFT) after participating in an EFT externship. In their supervision, Valencia notices that Humphrey conceptualizes and intervenes in almost all his cases through the lens of EFT and attachment theory. Coincidentally, EFT used to be Valencia's go-to approach when working with couples. Witnessing Humphrey's enthusiasm for EFT, Valencia thinks about her old self. Since now she has changed her worldview about therapy, she finds herself having a battle with Humphrey in terms of which direction to go, when the framework of therapy or intervention strategies are discussed. This leads to some tensions in their supervisory relationship. Whenever Humphrey limits his view of cases through the EFT lens, Valencia feels uncomfortable. Humphrey does not feel he is being supported—he is passionate about trying this new approach he just learned.

Valencia consults with her colleague David (also an IST supervisor) about her struggle. David also suggests Valencia focus the goal on promoting Humphrey's clinical competency rather than getting into a model battle. This conversation leads Valencia to reflect on the similarities and differences of IST and EFT, and shift the focus to help Humphrey use both and develop into a strong emotionally focused integrative systemic therapist.

In supervision with Humphrey, Valencia honestly shares her concerns about helping Humphrey become the best therapist that he can be. She tells Humphrey that she wants to support his goal of building expertise in EFT while she is concerned about a narrowed view of conceptualization from only one lens. Humphrey appreciates Valencia's concern, and they have a constructive discussion about how to use IST as a general theoretical framework while drawing techniques from EFT for now and gradually expanding using interventions from other approaches. In this way, they realign their supervision goal which allows for flexibility and individual development in the broader IST framework.

Training Background of the Integrative Systemic Supervisor

Each mental health subfield has some similar and some unique elements to training. The following section discusses how the specific training background of the supervisor interfaces with the development of competency as an IST supervisor in four of the mental health professions.

Counselor Education

Strengths

Counselor education programs have a strong emphasis in individual therapy theories. Many programs also have tracks in marriage and family counseling (MFC), and some clinical mental health counseling programs have a course in family and couple counseling.

Potential Missing Pieces

Common programs in departments of counselor education—such as clinical mental health counseling or school counseling—may have less emphasis on working with couples or families. Even in marriage and family counseling programs, for example, couple therapy training may be limited to a few approaches, leaving out a wide variety of ways of case conceptualization and intervention. Counselor education programs may also lack training in integration, particularly transtheoretical integration. There are exceptions. For instance, the Master of Arts in Clinical Mental Health Counseling at Gonzaga University has addressed this lack by offering a comprehensive and integrative "counseling matrix" model designed to help students transcend specific models, and to structure interventions (E. Bennett, personal communication, January 28, 2022).

Counselor Education Competencies Particularly Relevant to IST

For counselor education programs with a specialization in marriage, couple, and family counseling, specific standards cover foundations (e.g., history and theories), contextual factors (e.g., diagnosis, human sexuality, aging, violence, culture), and practice (e.g., systemic assessment, conceptualization, and interventions; CACREP, 2016). Other specialty areas such as clinical mental health counseling, addiction, career, or school counseling do not require the same systemic training.

SUGGESTIONS FOR THE COUNSELING SUPERVISOR'S DEVELOPMENT

The counselor educator or supervisor may want to evaluate how thorough their training background and clinical experience is in approaches to couple and family counseling. Additional training and supervision for the IST supervisor in couple and family counseling may be helpful. Reading or training in different types of integration—particularly transtheoretical—may also be crucial.

Marriage and Family Therapy

Strengths

Marriage and family therapy (or couple and family therapy) programs have a strong emphasis on systemic theories and approaches. All major systemic theories are generally covered as core components of training. Graduates from these programs should have a strong systemic lens from which to conceptualize client concerns.

Potential Missing Pieces

Marriage and Family Therapy programs may lack emphasis, training, or even any courses in individual approaches to psychotherapy. This may limit their drawing on any concepts and interventions from individual psychotherapy approaches. In addition, AAMFT competencies for supervision instructs supervisors to work within the model of the therapist. This may result in some unnecessary limitations on the therapist's development.

Marriage and Family Competencies Particularly Relevant to IST

The American Association for Marriage and Family Therapy (AAMFT) published their "Core Competencies" in 2004. AAMFT divides these competencies into six domains: (1) Admission to Treatment, (2) Clinical Assessment and Diagnosis, (3) Treatment Planning and Case Management, (4) Therapeutic Interventions, (5) Legal Issues, Ethics, and Standards, and (6) Research and Program Evaluation. Of note here, Domain 3 (Treatment Planning and Case Management) includes competencies such as effective models and integration of client feedback. Domain 4 (Therapeutic Interventions) includes comprehension of a "variety of individual and systemic therapeutic models."

Suggestions for the MFT Supervisor's Development

The IST supervisor coming from an MFT background may wish to assess their own level of training in individual models, and then pursue additional knowledge or training as needed. Like other fields, an understanding of the types of integration, with a focus on understanding the benefits and challenges of transtheoretical integration, is recommended.

Clinical and Counseling Psychology

Strengths

Clinical and counseling psychology programs often have strong training in individual approaches to psychotherapy. Some programs have general psychotherapy courses, and some have courses focused on a few major individual theories. Many of these programs cover the history of individual psychotherapy and the development and implementation of these approaches. Depending on the program, some have courses or an emphasis on couple and family therapy.

Potential Missing Pieces

While there are a wide variety of programs in psychology—including counseling and clinical psychology—there are no couple and family psychology training programs. In addition, family therapy training in psychology is rare. The American Psychological Association has one division devoted to systemic thinking—Division 43: The Society for Couple and Family Therapy—but this division is relatively small compared to other major divisions. A few programs in clinical or counseling psychology do offer some training in couple and family psychology (CFP), which are outlined by the division, from "Exposure" (offering one or two courses in CFP) or "Experience" (offering a practicum in addition to a few courses), to "Emphasis" (more than one practicum experience) or "Major area of study" (two or more years of courses, supervised practicum, and potential for major research projects in CFP (Society for Couple & Family Psychology)). Some programs offer training in psychotherapy integration, such as the course in psychotherapy integration in the clinical psychology program at Rutgers University, and the practicum experience in IST in the clinical psychology program at Northwestern University.

Psychology Competencies Particularly Relevant to IST

The American Psychological Association released the Revised Competence Benchmarks for Professional Psychology (2011) which outlines standards for readiness for practicum and internship, and entry to professional practice. One area—Systems—addresses the benchmark of systems change, involving working toward change at the institutional, community, or societal level, consistent with the IST web of human experience. Other competencies particularly relevant to IST supervision are the ability to apply scientific methods to intervention and reading feedback, and the utilization of case formulation for treatment planning which takes development and diversity into consideration. Although the benchmarks call for "fidelity to empirical models" which is not entirely consistent with an IST approach, the "flexibility to adapt where appropriate" is also noted. Stanton and Welsh (2011) completed a volume on competencies specific to couple and family psychology, including case conceptualization, intervention, consultation, and supervision from a systems perspective. Supervisors from a psychology background who find their training in psychology lacking in terms of systems theory may want to start with this book to evaluate their strengths and areas for continued learning as an integrative and systemic supervisor.

Suggestions for the Clinical or Counseling Psychology Supervisor's Development

The IST supervisor coming from a clinical or counseling psychology background may have training in specific individual approaches (e.g., cognitive behavioral therapy, psychodynamic, interpersonal), but may benefit from pursuing additional training in couple and family psychology. APA Division 43, for example, offers continuing education for training in systemic approaches. Some may also wish to pursue board certification as couple and family psychologists, through the American Board of Professional Psychology.

Clinical Social Work

Strengths

Social work as a field has a focus on broader systemic knowledge, up through the macro level. IST looks at strengths and constraints not only in the metaframeworks, but also on a multi-level system including community and society. Knowledge of these larger systems is one of the major strengths of a background of training in social work as an IST supervisor. Clinical social work programs also emphasize social justice, or an emphasis on improving or changing systems that impact clients.

Potential Missing Pieces

Even some clinical social work programs may have less emphasis on training specifically in psychotherapy. General clinical work at the micro level may not be emphasized to the same degree as other fields, including individual, couple, and family therapy.

Social Work Competencies Particularly Relevant to IST

The Council on Social Work Education outlines nine main competency areas, many of which are directly relevant for the practice of IST supervision. These include "research-informed practice," and assessment and intervention with clients from the individual to the community level. Coming from a social work background, an IST supervisor may be particularly ready to consider and work with community contexts that impact individual, couple, and family functioning.

Suggestions for the Social Work Supervisor's Development

Social workers can build on their macro-level competency by first assessing their level of therapy training at the micro level and the interaction between the macro and micro. If needed, IST supervisors in social work may wish to pursue additional therapy training in the areas needed (whether based in family systems or individual approaches). The social worker supervisor may find that their systemic knowledge lends itself well to thinking systemically at a smaller level with a couple or family.

Conclusion

In addition to developing the basic competencies of clinical supervision, supervisors must refine their competency in IST and be able to guide therapists through the essence diagram and other IST tools, as well as using IST for tracking the sequences in the therapist system. Self-of-the supervisor work also needs to take place. The supervisor needs to be aware of their inner process including their feelings, thoughts, and behaviors. and their interactions with the therapists within their settings and contexts. When the supervisor holds an open mind and is curious about how and why they think and feel, there is more room for reflection on how their reactions and beliefs may impact the supervisory relationship and client care. Depending on the training background of the supervisor, various strengths should be built upon and growth edges addressed. Overall, to improve one's supervision skills and outcomes, the supervisor needs to adopt a lifelong learning approach and take time and effort to deliberately reflect on one's supervision in a consistent manner. When the supervisor encounters difficulties that they cannot resolve, it is recommended that they seek supervision mentorship or peer consultation.

References

American Association for Marriage and Family Therapy. (2014). *Approved supervision designation: Standards handbook.* www.aamft.org/supervision/supervision. aspx.

American Association for Marriage and Family Therapy. (2004). *Marriage and family therapy core competencies*. www.aamft.org/common/Uploaded%20files/COAMFTE/Accreditation%20Resources/MFT%20Core%20Competencies%20(December%202004).pdf.

American Psychological Association. (2011). Competency benchmarks in professional psychology. www.apa.org/ed/graduate/competency.

American Psychological Association. (2014). *Guidelines for clinical supervision in health service psychology*. http://apa.org/about/policy/guidelines-supervision.pdf.

Aponte, H. J., & Carol Carlsen, J. (2009). An instrument for person-of-the-therapist supervision. *Journal of Marital and Family Therapy*, 35(4), 395–405. https://doi.org/10.1111/j.1752-0606.2009.00127.x.

Aponte H., & Kissel, K., (2016). "If I can grapple with this, I can truly be of use in the therapy room:" Using the therapist's own emotional struggles to facilitate effective therapy. *Journal of Marital and Family Therapy*, 40(2), 152–164. https://doi.org/10.1111/jmft.12011.

Baucom, D. H., Epstein, N. B., Kirby, J. S., & LaTaillade, J. L. (2015). Cognitive-behavioral couple therapy. In A. S. Gurman, J. L. Lebow, & D. K. Snyder (Eds.), *Clinical handbook of couple therapy* (5th ed., pp. 23–60). Guilford Press.

Bernard, J. M., & Goodyear, R. K. (2014). *Fundamentals of clinical supervision* (5th ed.). Pearson.

Breunlin, D. C., Pinsof, W., & Russell, W. P. (2011). Integrative problem-centered metaframeworks therapy I: Core concepts and hypothesizing. *Family Process*, 50(3), 293–313. https://doi.org/10.1111/j.1545-5300.2011.01362.x.

Breunlin, D. C. (1988). Oscillation theory and family development. In C. J. Falicov (Ed.), *Family transitions: continuity and change over the life cycle* (pp. 133–155). Guilford Press.

CACREP. (2016). 2016 CACREP standards. www.cacrep.org/for-programs/2016-cacrep-standards.

Chambers, A. L. (2019). African American couples in the 21st century: Using integrative systemic therapy (IST) to translate science into practice. *Family Process*, 58(3), 595–609. https://doi.org/10.1111/famp.12478.

De Shazer, S., Dolan, Y., Korman, H., Trepper, T., McCollum, E., & Berg, I. K. (2021). *More than miracles: The state of the art of solution-focused brief therapy*. Routledge.

Hardy, N. R., Brosi, M. W., & Gallus, K. L. (2019). Integrative systemic therapy: Lessons on collaboration and training for the 21st century. *Journal of Marital and Family Therapy*, 45(2), 206–218. https://doi.org/10.1111/jmft.12332.

He, Y., Hardy, N., Fisher, A., & Lokatama, I. (2023). The development of the Integrative Systemic Therapist. *Fokus På Familien*, 51(4), 315–331. https://doi.org/10.18261/fokus.51.4.4.

He, Y., Hardy, N., & Russell, W. (2021). Integrative systemic supervision: Promoting supervisees' theoretical integration in systemic therapy. *Family Process*, 61(1), 58–75. https://doi.org/10.1111/famp.12667.

He, Y., Fisher, A. R., Swanson, S. E., & Lebow, J. L. (2022). Integrative Systemic Therapy: Integrating individual, couple, and family therapy. *Australian and New Zealand Journal of Family Therapy*, 43(1), 9–21. https://doi.org/10.1002/anzf.1473.

Johnson, S. M. (2012). *The practice of emotionally focused couple therapy: Creating connection*. Routledge.

Lee, R. E., & Nelson, T. S. (2014). *The contemporary relational supervisor.* Routledge.

Morgan, M. M., & Sprenkle, D. H. (2007). Toward a common-factors approach to supervision. *Journal of Marital and Family Therapy*, 33(1), 1–17. https://doi.org/10.1111/j.1752-0606.2007.00001.x.

Pinsof, W. M., Breunlin, D. C., Russell, W. P., Lebow, J. L., Rampage, C., & Chambers, A. L. (2018). *Integrative systemic therapy: Metaframeworks for problem solving with individuals, couples, and families.* American Psychological Association.

Pinsof, W., Breunlin, D. C., Russell, W. P., & Lebow, J. A. Y. (2011). Integrative problem-centered metaframeworks therapy II: Planning, conversing, and reading feedback. *Family Process*, 50(3), 314–336. https://doi.org/10.1111/j.1545-5300.2011.01361.x.

Regas, S. J., Kostick, K. M., Bakaly, J. W., & Doonan, R. L. (2017). Including the self-of-the-therapist in clinical training. *Couple and Family Psychology: Research and Practice*, 6(1), 18. https://doi.org/10.1037/cfp0000073.

Russell, W. P., Breunlin, D. C., & Sahebi, B. (2023). *Integrative systemic therapy in practice: A clinician's handbook.* Routledge.

Russell, W. P., & Breunlin, D. C. (2019). Transcending therapy models and managing complexity: Suggestions from integrative systemic therapy. *Family Process*, 58(3), 641–655. https://doi.org/10.1111/famp.12482.

Russell, W.P., Pinsof, W., Breunlin, D., & Lebow, J. (2016). *Integrative problem-centered metaframeworks (IPCM) therapy.* In T. Sexton, & J. Lebow (Eds.), *Handbook of family therapy* (4th ed., pp. 530–544). Routledge.

Society for Couple and Family Psychology. (n.d.). Doctoral programs. APA Divisions. www.apadivisions.org/division-43/education-research/education/doctoral.

Stanton, M., & Welsh, R. (2011). *Specialty competencies in couple and family psychology.* Oxford University Press.

Timm, T. M., & Blow, A. J. (1999). Self-of-the-therapist work: A balance between removing restraints and identifying resources. *Contemporary Family Therapy*, 21(3), 331–351. https://doi.org/10.1023/A:1021960315503.

Chapter 6

The Development of the IST Therapist

The therapist plays a crucial role in clients' overall therapeutic journey. This role is realized through the therapeutic alliance that is built between therapist and clients. The alliance is quite possibly the strongest common factor for successful treatment outcomes (Flückiger et al., 2018). The degree to which a therapist is able to establish a strong *systemic* working alliance (Friedlander et al., 2018), provide a warm presence, and collaboratively direct the process of change cannot be understated. Nevertheless, the relationship that therapists create with their clients and how this impacts the treatment process is more complex than can be captured in alliance report measures. The therapist has a vital but intricate systemic role in addressing clients' problems, and the role of the therapist is not limited to the alliance alone, but also pertains to their effectiveness in collaborating with client systems to ultimately help them resolve their problem sequences and implement solution sequences. To do so, the therapist must be effective at identifying and defining clients' presenting problems, locating them within sequences, and establishing therapeutic contracts around important areas of focus in the therapy process. Therapists must be able to engage clients in the process of change, including relevant family members, in addressing their problems, lifting constraints to problem resolution, and ensuring lasting solution sequences are integrated into the client system. IST supervision, therefore, needs to center on building the therapist's capacity to build strong alliances with clients in the service of delivering effective therapeutic conversations that lead client systems into successful problem resolution.

Supervisors play a crucial role in helping therapists develop the knowledge, skills, and personal development necessary to be proficient in IST. This requires supervisors to be able to communicate and train therapists in the basic principles and applications of IST. It further requires supervisors to help therapists navigate consultation on specific cases and lean into IST's basic principles in a way that will help their clients. Supervisors must also recognize that therapists are part of a clinical system and play a role in creating clinical sequences that may be problematic or helpful (see Figure 1.4, The Therapy System). They must see the therapist through the lens of IST and help them learn to develop themselves using the tools of IST.

DOI: 10.4324/9781003146841-6

Yet the therapist is more than a robotic expression of IST—their person-hood makes them unique and gives variety and color to their therapeutic work. IST supervisors, then, must attend to the intersections between thera-pists embodying the principles of IST, developing their own unique gifts and talents as a therapist, and addressing their personal vulnerabilities and his-tories. This chapter addresses various aspects of supervision that deal directly with the therapist's development and role in therapy including the following: (a) applying IST tools to a therapist in the process of supervision, (b) identi-fying specific IST competencies therapists must develop, (c) helping therapists develop competencies across stages of skill acquisition using deliberate prac-tice, and (d) addressing and using the person of the IST therapist.

Applying IST Tools to the Therapist

The IST blueprint and essence are useful tools for framing the process of supervision in promoting therapists' competency development, advancing their systemic clinical position, and addressing the role of their personhood in the therapeutic encounter. Their application in the context of supervision showcases an isomorphic relationship to the therapy process. Just as they guide therapy, ensuring clients traverse their therapeutic journey effectively, they also guide the development of therapists. In supervision, the essence and blueprint are collaboratively leveraged to help therapists grow, which most often involves experiential learning opportunities in which specific case material that therapists bring to supervision is the primary point of discus-sion. Nevertheless, supervision may also deviate from case material to focus more broadly on the therapists' overall growth.

In contextualizing therapist development, the essence diagram is adapted to reflect a therapist's progression and areas of competency development. It provides both the supervisor and the therapist with a shared framework to understand where the therapist currently stands in their growth trajectory and what the subsequent steps might be. Specifically, a supervisor works with a therapist to identify a particular set of skills needing to be learned and then polished. They identify and work on the integration of these skills within their therapeutic systems and encounters. They then assess how well the therapist was able to implement those skills. If the therapist struggles to integrate the skills, they identify what constraints may be preventing their integration and what resources they can draw upon to help them improve. Lastly, they ensure the new skills are adequately implemented and con-sistently applied across their clinical casework.

In a similar way, the IST blueprint can be used to hypothesize which skills the therapist should attempt to develop either generally or for a specific case, and to explore various constraints and resources to their acquisition of that skill, including person-of-the-therapist factors. The supervisor and therapist then set plans for increasing skill development in these identified areas including strategies in and out of supervision. The supervisor converses with the therapist to facilitate skill acquisition and then gathers feedback about how well they are implementing the IST skills they are learning. In the process of conversing and feedback, the supervisor also attunes carefully to how well they are building a supervisory alliance and how well the therapist is responding to this supervision process, and they ensure conversations about the person of the therapist are handled with care.

As supervisors, it is critical to consider how to extend the principles of the blueprint and essence to include the direct therapist system, and not just the client system (see Figure 1.4). This is also the level at which supervisors have the most direct impact. Are there problems in the therapist system (e. g., between the therapist and the client)? If so, what are they? Are there problematic sequences the therapist has inadvertently created with their clients in attempting to address their problems? For example, therapists can over-function while their clients under-function, create coalitions with one member of a system against another member, pursue one member of the system on behalf of another member, or they can lose boundaries and over-disclose. Hence, it is useful for therapists and their supervisors to consider whether problematic sequences in the direct therapist system could explain slow or stalled progress. Once identified, they should explore possible ways to address these and form solution sequences in the therapy encounter. If unsuccessful, there may be constraints in the therapist or clients that prevent them from being able to resolve dynamics in the therapist–client system.

For example, therapists and clients may have similar or different cultural identities that may be representative, to either of them, of the dimensions of privilege and/or marginalization (Ratts et al., 2016). This lens could help identify constraints or resources that can emerge in the relationship between therapists and clients from each of their contexts of membership and the resulting dynamics created by intersecting cultural identities. In the direct therapist system, there may be any number of problematic sequences and constraints to explore, but there may also be solution sequences and resources that supervisors can help therapists identify as points of connection to leverage clinical progress with clients. Supervisors and therapists should evaluate the direct therapist system regularly and work to ensure the maintenance of effective therapeutic alliances and clinical progress. A parallel process should also be evaluated in terms of the supervisor–therapist system (see Chapter 5). It will be difficult for therapists to grow in the context of supervision and for supervisors to guide therapists when there are problematic sequences and constraints within this system.

Finally, the IST tools are also used by the supervisor to address self-of-the-therapist dynamics that emerge across the course of supervision and with particular cases. In this regard, the blueprint is quite useful. A supervisor may use the web of human experience to identify aspects of the therapist that are intersecting with their development or with their casework. For example, a supervisor could bring up the gender metaframe-work when a therapist who identifies as a woman and has experienced trauma from men is triggered by a client who identifies as a man and tries to dominate the direction of therapy. A supervisor can easily go down the planning matrix (see Figure 1.3, IST Planning Matrix) with a therapist to identify strategies they may apply to themselves as it relates to an internal mental or emotional constraint that has prevented them from connecting with or handling difficulties with their clients.

Therapists don't have to know all the models or strategies to do this. Working from the principle of equifinality (that the same outcome can be reached through multiple pathways), it may be that a strategy (e.g., restruc-turing cognitions; doing genograms) from any planning metaframework (e.g., meaning/emotion; family of origin) may lift the therapist's constraint. Even an open acknowledgment of the personhood process that is occurring can go a long way. Nevertheless, as the therapist develops, they may find value or even necessity in learning other strategies (e.g., parts-work; integrating spiri-tuality) from other planning metaframeworks (e.g. internal representation; self). We will revisit in more detail how IST addresses and promotes person-of-the-therapist development later in the chapter.

IST Competencies in the Developing Therapist

It is crucial for supervisors to help therapists learn and develop the basic competencies of IST as they work to become effective therapists. Some of these skills are common across various training contexts and models (e.g., collaboration), yet IST competencies bring many tools together from various models and approaches into a comprehensive and organized set of skills. This is invaluable as many therapists have the experience of being siloed into one or two models, and, hence, their skills are constrained to develop within them. The complexity of therapy requires a broader set of skills than any one model can provide, alongside a deep focus on the therapists' own development. Based on the tools of IST (essence and blueprint) and its pil-lars and guidelines, we describe a set of IST competencies that supervisors can help therapists develop.

Developing Competencies with the Essence Diagram of IST

Supervisors ensure that therapists are well versed in and following the essence diagram of IST. This includes more than just making sure therapists follow the step-by-step process of therapy, but that they have a deep understanding of the basic tasks within each step, and that they can apply each of them effectively. As supervisors observe or discuss therapists' clinical material, they try to identify generally where therapists are at in this essence diagram and how well they are executing the tasks of that step. On the other hand, they should also consider whether therapists should locate themselves somewhere else in the diagram and explain why they are not there. This allows the supervisor to train therapists in the skills of advancing therapy in the correct way and at an effective pace. For example, it is common for new therapists to feel compelled to find solutions to clients' problems before they have a sufficient grasp on them. It may be necessary to guide therapists to first get a very clear understanding and collaborative definition of the problems, including a clear description of their manifestation in sequences, before introducing possible solutions.

Further, the supervisor's use of the essence allows therapists to consider their role beyond delivering a simple set of interventions or applying dialogical tools in the room. They see their function as moving therapy along a course of treatment that helps clients get unstuck from their problems to finally maintain new solutions. Therapists are trained to do this by putting emphasis on and revisiting the effectiveness of the initial therapeutic contracts, problem definitions, sequences, and attempts at implementing solutions sequences. Therapists are also more able to identify constraints and access more complicated interventions for handling more difficult problems. Therapists bring together a holistic understanding of a client system's set of problems and identify a comprehensive set of tools that enable their clients to maintain the solutions they need to be successful long-term. Therefore, supervisors should continuously be helping therapists think in terms of therapeutic traction and progress for clients as opposed to only worrying about their performance of specific interventions.

Nevertheless, as therapists do seek a repertoire of effective interventions and a deepening of these skills, the supervisor helps therapists choose clinically relevant models, strategies, and interventions that may be useful for their case work and overall development. For example, therapists working with whole families may find advantages in studying various strategies and techniques from structural family therapy, including enactments and restructuring. IST supervisors teach therapists to appreciate the vast library of interventions that can be drawn from models in couple therapy, family therapy, individual therapy, group therapy, etc.

Developing Competencies in the IST Blueprint

The IST blueprint provides supervisors with a vast repository of knowledge and practice distilled from the many models of psychotherapy. It enables supervisors to help therapists identify and develop the various skills that enable their use of the IST essence.

Hypothesizing Competencies

Supervisors help therapists make sense of and form ideas about client systems and their problem sequences, constraints, resources, and potential solution sequences. They help therapists learn to work and rework their hypotheses about client systems. They ensure therapists are well versed in diverse theories, research, and clinical assessment tools that aid in the formation of their hypotheses. For example, supervisors train therapists to use the web of human experience as a heuristic device to aid their thinking about their client's constraints and resources. Supervisors should assess therapists' ability to think in terms of sequences and to hold complexity. Supervisors can workshop with therapists these skills, such as by having therapists fill in the web-of-human-experience diagram for a particular client. Hypothesizing skills should also be transitional to helping therapists develop ways to test their hypotheses with their clients. In other words, therapists must learn to connect their ideas to practical application for a client system's treatment plan.

Planning Competencies

Therapists are aided by supervisors in knowing the set of strategies and interventions that might best address the specific issues clients are bringing to therapy. Supervisors share from their own repository of knowledge and skill sets, but they also aid therapists in the process of making decisions about what they might be able to do to address their clients' problems. Supervisors train therapists to use the IST planning matrix to help guide their planning. As a thinking tool, it does not specify exactly what a therapist should do or what order of interventions they should follow, but it does provide general guidance in the decision-making process. Supervisors could use this diagram and have therapists pick spots that seem particularly relevant for their clients, which can then lead to brainstorming more specific plans. Ultimately, supervisors must train therapists to make informed decisions and proceed with them, recognizing that therapy involves trial and error. Further, the planning metaframeworks also provide avenues for supervisors to address key areas where a therapist may be able to identify core strengths (e.g., emotion-centered interventions) in their intervention skills or key areas needing further skill development (e.g., system and action oriented interventions).

Conversing Competencies

The heart of therapy and the most significant role of the therapist is in the actual therapeutic conversation with clients. Supervisors give special attention to how therapists are using therapeutic encounters to build a relationship with their client(s), develop an understanding of their system, engage them in the process of change, and structure their therapy. The therapist must be skilled in conducting conversations that lead to a collaborative definition of the problem and a shared understanding of the constraints and solutions. Supervisors ensure therapists are skilled in a diverse set of conversational elements including turn-taking, questions, statements, directives, silence, nonverbal communication, the different language for action, meaning, and emotion, as well as alternatives to talk therapy, including play or art. These conversational moves will vary from the type of problems being worked with, the age of clients, and their cultural background.

As these are skills that take practice and fine-tuning to develop, the supervisor is vigilant in observing these skills and providing guidance to improve them. There are many reasons why therapists struggle to know how and when to employ particular conversational moves. For example, some therapists get uncomfortable with silence, and supervisors may guide them to hold silence when therapeutically beneficial—such as when clients are processing a new idea or emotion. Further still, many therapists lack a multicultural understanding of the role these differing conversational moves may have for clients (Sue et al., 2022). For example, clients from some racial groups may see silence as a form of respect. Others may expect more directives and statements. Some new therapists often struggle to position themselves beyond questioning and listening, but many cultural frameworks expect more active leadership from therapists. Many minority groups are often more finely in tune with nonverbal communication and may interpret some forms of nonverbal communication from therapists as representations of their power or privilege (Sue et al., 2022). Additionally, supervisors also help therapists to navigate the place of self-disclosure in therapy by balancing the client system's cultural background, a therapist's own purpose of self-disclosure, and whether the disclosure ultimately accrues to the benefit of the client system.

Finally, it is crucial that therapists develop a personal style for relating to their clients. For example, some therapists are fantastic at asking well-crafted and well-placed questions, some may be great conceptualizers and will be able to offer powerful statements. Other therapists are great at emotion and directing clients to deeper and softer emotional states. Here, the supervisor highlights and discusses the way the therapist shows up as a person in the room and leverages their unique talents, personalities, and skills in relating to and helping clients. They also identify blocks to their ability to connect or stay present with clients. For example, some therapists were trained by their family of origin to avoid emotion, and it may take work in supervision to help the therapist learn to tolerate difficult emotions of their clients.

Feedback Competencies

It is important that supervisors help therapists learn how to determine if their work is actually helpful to their clients and their problem resolution. There are a number of skills that are useful for therapists to develop to make these determinations and lead to revisions in their conceptualization and treatment. First, therapists must demonstrate an ability to read feedback from clients, which can happen by collecting useful information from clients during intake, making observations during sessions, and listening to their own reactions to client information. Supervisors should also train therapists to learn to share their feedback with clients and check to see whether that feedback matches that of the clients or can be integrated into the client's new understanding. They also train them to receive feedback from clients regarding how clients perceive them and the work that is occurring. Finally, supervisors can help therapists use empirical and systematic assessments as a form of feedback about clients' progress as well as about the alliance. Some examples of feedback systems that collect useful data on various measures may include the Systemic Therapy Inventory of Change (STIC; Pinsof, 2017), the MFT Practice Research Network (MFT-PRN; Johnson et al., 2017), and the Outcome Rating Scale and Session Rating Scale (ORS and SRS; Campbell & Hemsley, 2009). Checking in with therapists regularly on their use of these tools and helping them properly analyze their data will increase therapist's competence in using feedback.

Developing Competencies in the IST Pillars

Supervisors must work with therapists to adopt a unifying and transcending conceptual and foundational framework to orient themselves to integrative and systemic therapy. The five pillars of IST (epistemological, ontological, sequences, constraint, causality) provide this overarching view of therapy, dealing more broadly with how a therapist approaches the whole therapeutic enterprise. These pillars were recently identified as a cohesive paradigm for advancing systemic family research (Whittaker et al., 2023). As these pillars deal less with specific therapist behaviors and more with the philosophical and paradigmatic lenses therapists have about therapy, they may require focused conversational exchanges between supervisors and therapists about how they are working through their own beliefs and coming to understand the balanced, integrative, and multi-systemic approach of IST.

Epistemological Competencies

The epistemological pillar addresses the stance a therapist takes regarding how objective or subjective reality is. Supervisors ensure the therapist can balance the notions of objective and subjective realities by encouraging therapists to stand in a space of "partial and progressive knowing" where they are humble in recognizing what they do not yet know but are trying to learn and understand about what may be real. There is value in the notions of both objective and subjective views of reality. For example, siblings may each share divergent perspectives with their family therapist about how their parents are involved in their lives. One sibling may feel the parents are too intrusive with expectations that are too high, while the other experiences the parents as uninvolved or uninterested. Both perspectives are valid subjective realities. They may also be valid representations of their experiences objectively since many parents treat their children differently. While this initial information gives a powerful sense of what different children are experiencing, and therefore opens the door to more understanding about how this might be affecting them and problems in the family more generally, it is, nevertheless, continuing to breed problematic clashes of reality between members of the family. Regardless of what the objective reality actually is, the therapist gathers sufficient information to more closely approximate a shared reality that can be collaboratively determined and useful to addressing the problems in therapy. It may be that children's perspectives are affected by different expectations each child has for parents. It may be that the parents are intrusive in some contexts and distant in others. IST therapists work with all perspectives and aim to develop mutual understanding and shared agreements.

Supervisors help therapists identify the powerful experience of subjective reality in their clients and help navigate colliding realities between clients in a relationship system and between themselves as the therapist and their clients. While honoring these subjective realities, they aim to create points of collaborative understanding and shared meaning and aim to resolve tensions by finding a deeper understanding of objective and systemic realities occurring within, between, and around the clients. Supervisors check in with therapists about how they are positioning themselves in their therapeutic role with clients and help them find balance between expert and non-expert stances. This includes cultural sensitivity towards clients' preferences for therapists to practice in either expert or non-expert roles. Supervisors open dialogue with therapists about their own worldviews and how they personally wrestle with this tension in their therapeutic work. They guide therapists toward an appreciation of the balanced view of reality IST promotes.

Ontological Competencies

The ontological pillar addresses the nature of things. Applied to therapy, it states a position about the nature of human interaction—namely, that it is systemic. Supervisors help therapists think systemically (Stanton & Welsh, 2012). Many models direct therapists to think about their clients' problems according to their approach or theory. IST instead embraces multiple perspectives to understanding clients' issues. This approach is systemic in that it considers several contributing interacting forces on the functioning of a client system, whether that be an individual, couple, or family. Supervisors ensure therapists are not locked into one way of thinking and conceptualizing. Nevertheless, IST values the rich history and various principles of systems theory itself (Bertalanffy, 1975), especially how the theory has been applied to understanding families (Bowen, 1978; Minuchin, 1974) and other contextual layers of influence (Bronfenbrenner, 2005). A systemic view allows therapists to see clearly the intricacy in a client's set of problems. Supervisors ensure therapists know and can identify these various systemic processes in context (e.g., behavior in context, subsystems, function of behavior, homeostasis and morphogenesis, to name a few). Some therapists are not initially trained in systems theory or to work with multiple parties in the clinical room, and those who are trained this way still often struggle to think and work systemically. In these cases, supervisors must be vigilant in exploring therapists' systemic hypothesizing and treatment planning. If lacking, supervisors can recommend readings in systems theory and promote systemic conceptualizing about therapists' cases.

Sequences Competencies

The systemic view enables therapists to capture the totality of the canvas of a client system. To make systemic therapy manageable, IST works with that tapestry by picking relevant threads of it that constitute sequences. Hence, supervisors teach therapists to identify patterned and repetitious cycles of action, meaning, and emotion. They ensure that therapists are continuously looking for problematic sequences in their clients and that they are able to find replacement solution sequences. This often involves brainstorming with therapists what those problem and solution sequences could be. It also involves training therapists to collaborate with clients in the process of identifying both problem and solution sequences. Watching videos of sessions is one of the most effective ways to sharpen therapists' observational skills so they can read the feedback that constitutes a part of the sequence.

Constraint Competencies

Although many therapies work from the assumption that some deficit within a person explains problems within a client system, IST leans more toward the assumption of resilience and that difficulties changing are best explained by constraints to resolving patterns. Supervisors help therapists understand that problem resolution for clients is not always easy or simple and they guide therapists in how to be patient with the process. They help therapists recognize that sequences are embedded within a web of constraints and that problems are not found by identifying some deficit within one person. Supervisors aid therapists to move from asking the question "What causes this problem?" to asking the question "What keeps the problem from being solved?" Because inner psychological explanations of personal and relationship functioning are so common in the culture, supervisors must observe carefully how these beliefs might emerge and how conversations might become centered around the first question. They must discuss frequently the systemic paradigm and the reality of multiple constraints to clients being able to change something in a complex system. They aid the therapist in shifting their hypothesizing questions about the client and their conversational strategies with the client to help generate a more useful understanding of the problems and the potential for change.

Causality Competencies

Causality investigates how the various causes lead to particular unwanted or wanted effects in a client system. An IST supervisor should enable therapists to think about the causes of a client's problems in circular, non-linear terms. It is easy for clients and therapists to find a single linear cause to their problems (e.g., dysfunctional partner, early trauma). While therapists should take many of these factors into account as differential causes with varying degrees of influence, therapists should continuously see and work with reinforcing patterns that maintain problems and constrain solutions from being enacted. Supervisors help therapists hold to views of circular and differential causality.

Developing Competencies in the IST Guidelines

Like the IST pillars, the 12 guidelines of IST are a useful tool for supervisors to promote important ways therapists should orient their work when practicing IST. Therapists should be able to ensure their interventions are always linked, in some way, to the problems clients have identified as important to their therapy. They should assume client systems have resources to lift constraints and implement solution sequences with direct and minimal input or be aware when those resources are insufficient. Therapists attune to clients' sociocultural contexts of membership and social justice issues in the problem-solving process. They should recognize that assessment and intervention are recursive and ongoing processes, and should always be open to new information and willing to adapt their approach. They should see their primary task as replacing problem sequences with solution sequences. Therapists should be trained to be informed by empirical data and science in order to be maximally effective and efficient. They should be willing to share their knowledge, skills, and expertise with their clients as readily as clients can integrate them. They should aim to be cost-effective and begin with less expensive and more direct interventions but be willing to move toward more involved interventions if needed. As much as possible, therapists should attempt interventions in an interpersonal context so as to ensure greater likelihood of solution maintenance. They should generally focus first on here-and-now issues but progress to complex and past issues as needed. They should be flexible and shift their approach when interventions fail.

Finally, therapists should prioritize the therapeutic alliance over specific interventions unless this priority compromises the effectiveness of therapy. Supervisors can keep all these guidelines in mind as they assess and promote the ongoing development of therapists.

The Promotion of Competency Development in the IST Therapist

Various schemas explain the process of skill acquisition that can be applied to our understanding of the course of competency development in the IST therapist. For example, the Dreyfus model (Benner, 2004) suggests that competencies are developed across five general stages: novice, advanced beginner, competent, proficient, and expert. It is useful to locate where a therapist may be in their course of learning IST and how to best help them in that zone of development. Therapists in the novice stage have a basic understanding of IST but lack practical experience. Role-playing and supervised practice sessions drawing on IST skills are useful at this stage. Advanced beginners have some experience conducting therapy sessions using IST but still focus mostly on basic skills like identifying and articulating problem sequences, and struggle to handle more nuanced and complex constraints. Observing experienced therapists, participating in group supervision sessions, and receiving feedback on their sessions are useful at this stage.

In the competent stage, therapists use IST more independently and start to develop their own personal style, integrating different metaframeworks and skills for various types of situations. They may still struggle with highly complex client systems. Advanced workshops, case discussions, and peer supervision are useful at this stage. Proficient therapists have a deep understanding of IST and are able to seamlessly adapt their approach to the unique needs of a client system. They are able to integrate feedback from clients, and adjust their therapeutic approach fluidly, relying on both intuition and high-level conceptualizing. Therapists in this stage need continuous professional development, exploring niche areas within IST, and the opportunity to mentor less experienced therapists. Finally, experts have mastered the craft of IST and possess a deep intuitive understanding of client systemic dynamics and the broad repertoire of interventions. They handle challenging cases with ease, being able to innovate and introduce new therapeutic moves. Experts lead workshops, contribute to IST scholarship, and supervise other therapists.

Another useful framework for training IST therapists is deliberate practice, which is a focused and purposeful practice aimed at specific areas of improvement (Anders Ericsson, 2008). Deliberate practice involves multiple training strategies that increase the therapist's proficiency in a set of skills (Rousmaniere, 2016). As it relates to IST, deliberate practice would begin by identifying specific IST skills the therapist wishes to master. One tool for identifying areas for improvement is demonstrating therapy sessions (such as in live, video, or audio observation) and exploring areas of IST needing improvement. For instance, a therapist may want to improve their skills in communicating a directive to help implement a solution sequence. Therapists would then engage in structured practice sessions focusing on the identified IST skill, which can include role-playing with supervisors and peers. Therapists should be pushed slightly beyond their comfort zone during practice scenarios so as to ensure their continuous growth in IST. Repetition with variation allows the therapist to generalize the IST skill to different client scenarios, which is especially important regarding the diversity of various therapeutic contexts (individual, couple, family).

After each practice session, the therapist receives feedback. In a training setting, this could come from a supervisor or peer. The feedback should be specific and centered on the IST skill, pointing out both strengths and areas needing improvement. Therapists should reflect on their performance, integrate feedback, and identify strategies for further improvement. As IST skills are honed through deliberate practice, they should be integrated into actual therapy sessions. Subsequent feedback from these sessions can then inform future rounds of deliberate practice. Given the evolving nature of therapy and individual client needs, therapists should continuously identify new IST skills or techniques to master, and keep the cycle of deliberate practice ongoing. This structured approach to skill enhancement has been applied to many different models or modalities of therapy (see APA's 16-book series on the Essentials of Deliberate Practice) but has never been articulated for IST. When applied to IST training, it ensures that therapists not only gain experience but also continuously refine and elevate their therapeutic skills to meet the diverse and complex needs of their clients.

Vignette

Vivian is a 25-year-old Asian American therapist who has been seeing clients for six months at a community mental health clinic. She meets weekly with her supervisor, Maria, to discuss her cases and receive guidance on her development as an IST therapist. In recent supervision sessions, Maria has noticed that Vivian tends to jump into giving advice without first collaboratively exploring the clients' problems and locating them within a problem sequence.

In their next supervision meeting, Maria decides to address this issue:

MARIA: Vivian, I've noticed you move quick to offering solutions before fully defining the problem. Can you tell me more about what's behind that?

VIVIAN: Well, when clients tell me about their problems, I get anxious that I need to help them as fast as possible. So, I skip over really understanding the problem and its connections and just give my advice. I tend to jump in with my own ideas about what the root issue is and how they can address it.

MARIA: I appreciate you being open about that. I know you want to help your clients, but it's important we don't make assumptions or give advice before truly understanding their perspectives about their problems and locating them within sequences—doing so will give you greater clarity on where you can intervene with solutions.

VIVIAN: I see what you mean. My clients may feel like I'm not really getting the full picture and my solutions won't actually help if I don't grasp the broader patterns going on.

MARIA: Exactly. I'd like to help you improve your hypothesizing skills so you can better locate problems in sequences first. Can I suggest some ideas that we could try out in supervision to work on this?

VIVIAN: Yes, please. I want to improve in this area.

Together, they map out a plan to help Vivian adopt a more collaborative stance, enhancing her hypothesizing and better locating problems within sequences before planning advice. Maria suggests role-plays where she acts as a client with an ambiguous concern and Vivian practices exploring the issue from the client's viewpoint, securing an agreement from the client about what the problem is, and then asking questions that generate clarity about how the problem plays out in a sequence. Vivian will also track in each session whether she gave solutions prematurely without a clear and full description from the client. They will process these instances in supervision. If Vivian continues to struggle, Maria will explore if Vivian's constraints, such as her family-of-origin experiences, impact her need to provide quick solutions. The goal is for Vivian to learn to conceptualize collaboratively and offer solutions only after she has fully identified problem sequences.

In subsequent sessions, Maria checks in on Vivian's progress and provides feedback. After several weeks of deliberate practice, Vivian shows improvement in allowing clients to define their own problems and refraining from unsolicited advice. Vivian feels encouraged that she is developing competence as a systemic therapist through this collaborative approach.

Developing the Self of the IST Therapist

Encompassed in every therapist system is the therapist as person. The person of the therapist is a fundamental part of that system and all of its clinical encounters. IST opens the door to identify and work with the personal themes of strength and vulnerability that therapists bring to their work with clients and to their overall development as therapists. These themes may become explicitly integrated in supervision and can be brought up by either the therapist or supervisor in a sensitive and collaborative manner. Nevertheless, the supervisor is clear in the boundaries between self-work as it relates to the therapist's role as a therapist and self-work they may need to do in their own therapy. IST integrates many aspects of the Person-of-the-Therapist model (POTT; Aponte & Kissil, 2016) by helping therapists identify "signature themes" that may be intersecting in their therapy. Nevertheless, as an integrative approach, IST also draws ideas from various other scholars who have contributed to the use of self in therapy (see Baldwin 2013). Theoretical lenses such as attachment, differentiation, family systems, object relations, internal family systems, etc. may all prove useful applications for the therapist to understand themselves as a person and the way that selfhood intersects with their therapeutic work. Supervisors can help navigate conversations about these themes, but are cautious not to apply labels (e.g., poorly differentiated, anxiously attached) or diagnoses (e.g., depressed) to the therapist, but rather open the door for therapists to discuss their ideas and explore them further on their own. These signature themes—that are best identified by the therapist (e.g., sense of inadequacy in the presence of father figures in therapy)—can be integrated into conversations about the clinical work itself as well as about the development of the therapist.

Further, IST offers a structured process by which supervisors address selfhood themes as a therapist develops competency in IST and works with their cases. The IST supervisor does not call out a selfhood theme out of nowhere just because they think a therapist has a personal issue. Of course, a therapist in supervision can bring up selfhood issues or dynamics at any point in the process of supervision, and sometimes they may be seemingly unrelated to a particular case or skill. In these situations, the supervisor should carefully connect the discussion back to a focus on the therapist's overall development or with specific cases they are working with. Either way, the supervisor generally begins the process of identifying selfhood dynamics with a therapist by a focus on the therapist within the clinical system.

When it comes to particular cases, the supervisor looks at where the therapist and client may or may not have a system that is working well for therapeutic progress. This can then open the door to an exploration of how the therapist's role in the system is affected by various selfhood themes that may be arising in the process. Sometimes this may involve a particular therapeutic episode in which the therapist was clearly flustered or upset, or it may involve a series of interactions where the therapist was unable to effectively connect or intervene due to a selfhood issue. In either case, the supervisor keenly connects the selfhood dynamic first to sequences in the therapist–client (clinical) system and explores how a signature theme may be a key aspect of the pattern. Initially, simply drawing attention to this may be sufficient for the therapist to identify what is going on a find new alternatives. The supervisor, however, may need to explore more specifically what the theme is about and why it might be showing up in the way it is, as well as identify some specific ways to show up differently, and thereby modify the clinical sequence. Thus, in discussing selfhood themes as they relate to cases, the supervisor aims for some modification in the clinical system and traction in the therapist's work on signature themes.

Sometimes selfhood themes become larger constraints to the clinical system such that supervisors must gauge carefully whether therapists need to do further work in supervision or in their own therapy to address their signature themes and lift that particular constraint. Further, the supervisor should understand that selfhood work around case material is usually and often not solely concerning one or a few cases for the therapist, but importantly also about the therapist's overall development. Therapists want to be effective and know that these personal issues are important to all of their clinical work, and sometimes even to the very notion of being a professional in the field of therapy. Supervisors are open to these conversations about how therapists are feeling about their work as therapists, about being therapists, and about the challenges of having their own issues brought out through the process. Sometimes discussions about therapist burnout and compassion fatigue may be merited in the supervision process. It can be helpful to also tap into personal or contextual resources that help therapists bolster energy and motivation to address burnout and signature theme dynamics.

Another way the supervisor can elicit particular selfhood themes is in the process of IST skill development. There may be particular reasons why a therapist is struggling to develop a particular IST skill that may be related to their own history, personality, trauma, etc. For example, some therapists may struggle with building collaborative alliances between family members when they feel compelled to side with one of them who is experiencing relationship distress similar to distressing situations in the therapist's own past. Thus, the IST skills of balancing alliances may be thwarted. When supervisors and therapists recognize these barriers to skill development, they place emphasis on developing the skill in contexts that are most difficult for the therapist. If needed, this can then open the door to further exploration on the signature theme, but sometimes it is sufficient to honor and recognize what is happening, and then work to develop the skill in the context of the theme. Whether by processing cases or exploring specific IST skills, there are many openings for supervisors to elicit and draw out those themes that may be complicating clinical progress or therapist development. However, it is important for supervisors to also be strengths based in their approach and elicit, notice, and highlight the selfhood resiliencies that are manifested throughout their casework and development. Doing so can help therapists lean into those strengths, leverage them in difficult moments, and use them to aid their process of addressing their vulnerabilities.

Vignette

Mark is a 30-year-old White male graduate student completing his clinical practicum at the university's training clinic. He meets weekly with his supervisor, Juanita, a 45-year-old Latina professor, to discuss his work with clients. In recent sessions, Juanita has noticed that Mark becomes defensive when clients challenge him or express frustration about something that occurred in therapy. She decides to explore this pattern in their next supervision meeting.

JUANITA: Mark, I've noticed you seem to get defensive when clients question you or express frustration about the therapeutic process. Can you tell me more about what comes up for you in those moments?

MARK: You're right, I do get defensive and want to justify myself. I think it makes me feel like I've failed or done something wrong as a therapist.

JUANITA: It's very normal to have those feelings when someone expresses displeasure. What do you think underlies those feelings of inadequacy?

MARK: Now that you mention it, I was often criticized harshly by my father growing up. I absorbed this sense that any mistake meant total failure.

JUANITA: It seems your personal history may be shaping how you receive criticism and frustration as a therapist. This offers us an opportunity to explore how your past intersects with your clinical work.

MARK: I'd really appreciate any help responding better so I can stay present with clients.

Juanita suggests they do some role-plays where she gives critical feedback and Mark practices self-reflection and non-defensive responses. She also recommends Mark journal about his emotions after difficult sessions for them to process together. Over time, Mark becomes better at identifying his triggers and remains grounded when clients express frustration. He is grateful to have a supervisor who helps him develop self-awareness so he can better use his whole self effectively as a therapist-in-training.

As IST supervisors help therapists learn about the role of their own self-hood in therapeutic encounters, therapists may grow in multiple ways. They can progressively come to terms with aspects of themselves they must address more fully or regulate more diligently. They may increase in self-compassion about their vulnerabilities, even seeing the ways their own humanity connects them to the humanity of their clients. They may find ways to adapt their previous weaknesses into strengths or learn to compensate for their limitations by leveraging other resources in their personality. Regardless, therapists in IST are progressively working to bring their best and full self to the therapy, ultimately seeing therapy as a relational and human encounter that requires depth of presence and compassion, not just science and technique. As Michael Nichols once stated:

The more we talk about techniques, the greater the danger of seeing family therapy as a purely technical enterprise. Studying families is like solving a riddle; the art of treating them is to relieve suffering and anguish. The job of the theoretician is to decode and decipher, which requires theory and ingenuity. The job of the therapist is healing, which requires theory but also conviction, perseverance, and caring. Treating families isn't just a matter of theory and technique, it's also an act of love.

(Nichols, 2016, p. 267)

Conclusion

The therapist is the fulcrum of IST practice, and thus IST supervision must deliberately explore the therapist's role, development, and experiences in IST. In this chapter, we explored the application of IST tools (essence and blueprint) as isomorphic devices to the process of supervision including the development of therapist, the therapist in the clinical system, and the self-of-the-therapist. Then we discussed the specific competencies of IST that supervisors must ensure therapists are developing in the essence, blueprint, pillars, and guidelines of IST. We explored how to see therapists along a developmental trajectory of skill acquisition and how therapists can use deliberate practice methods to enhance their skill development. Finally, we closely examined the self-of-the-therapist and how signature themes intersect with therapy itself. Ultimately, we close with the understanding that therapy is a human-to-human conversation where therapists must bring their full selfhood to the healing work of therapy.

References

Anders Ericsson, K. (2008). Deliberate practice and acquisition of expert performance: A general overview. *Academic Emergency Medicine*, 15(11), 988–994. https://doi.org/10.1111/j.1553-2712.2008.00227.x.

Aponte, H. J., & Kissil, K. (Eds.). (2016). *The person of the therapist training model: Mastering the use of self*. Routledge.

Baldwin, M. (Ed.). (2013). *The use of self in therapy*. Routledge.

Benner, P. (2004). Using the Dreyfus model of skill acquisition to describe and interpret skill acquisition and clinical judgment in nursing practice and education. *Bulletin of Science, Technology & Society*, 24(3), 188–199. https://doi.org/10.1177/0270467604265061.

Bertalanffy, L. von (1975). *Perspectives on general system theory: Scientific–philosophical studies*. Braziller.

Bowen, M. (1978). *Family therapy in clinical practice*. Jason Aronson.

Bronfenbrenner, U. (2005). *Making human beings human: Bioecological perspectives on human development*. Sage.

Campbell, A., & Hemsley, S. (2009). Outcome Rating Scale and Session Rating Scale in psychological practice: Clinical utility of ultra-brief measures. *Clinical Psychologist*, 13(1), 1–9. https://doi.org/10.1080/13284200802676391.

Flückiger, C., Del Re, A. C., Wampold, B. E., & Horvath, A. O. (2018). The alliance in adult psychotherapy: A meta-analytic synthesis. *Psychotherapy*, *55*(4), 316–340. https://doi.org/10.1037/pst0000172.

Friedlander, M.L., Escudero, V., Welmers-van de Poll, M.J., & Heatherington, L. (2018). Meta-analysis of the alliance-outcome relation in couple and family therapy. *Psychotherapy 55*, 356–371. https://doi.org/10.1037/pst0000161.

Johnson, L. N., Miller, R. B., Bradford, A. B., & Anderson, S. R. (2017). The marriage and family therapy practice research network (MFT-PRN): Creating a more perfect union between practice and research. *Journal of Marital and Family Therapy*, *43*(4), 561–572. https://doi.org/10.1111/jmft.12238.

Minuchin, S. (1974). *Families and family therapy*. Harvard University Press.

Nichols, M. P. (2016). *Family therapy: Concepts and methods*, 11th ed. Pearson Higher Education.

Pinsof, W. M. (2017). The Systemic Therapy Inventory of Change—STIC: A multi-systemic and multi-dimensional system to integrate science into psychotherapeutic practice. In T. Tilden & B. Wampold (Eds.), *Routine outcome monitoring in couple and family therapy: The empirically informed therapist* (pp. 85–101). European Family Therapy Association Series. Springer. https://doi.org/10.1007/978-3-319-50675-3_5.

Ratts, M. J., Singh, A. A., Nassar-McMillan, S., Butler, S. K., & McCullough, J. R. (2016). Multicultural and social justice counseling competencies: Guidelines for the counseling profession. *Journal of Multicultural Counseling and Development*, *44*(1), 28–48. https://doi.org/10.1002/jmcd.12035.

Rousmaniere, T. (2016). *Deliberate practice for psychotherapists: A guide to improving clinical effectiveness*. Routledge.

Stanton, M., & Welsh, R. (2012). Systemic thinking in couple and family psychology research and practice. *Couple and Family Psychology: Research and Practice*, *1*(1), 14–30. https://doi.org/10.1037/a0027461.

Sue, D. W., Sue, D., Neville, H. A., & Smith, L. (2022). *Counseling the culturally diverse: Theory and practice*. John Wiley & Sons.

Whittaker, K., Stokkebekk, J., Lorås, L., & Tilden, T. (2023). Researching what we practice—The paradigm of systemic family research: Part 2. *Family Process*, *62*(3), 961–975. https://doi.org/10.1111/famp.12921.

Chapter 7

From Classroom to Clinic

How a Curriculum Shapes the Educational Foundation of the Supervisory Relationship

When a supervisor embarks on working with a therapist, the therapist brings a set of assets to the supervisory experience. These assets include the characteristics of the therapist, the accumulated clinical experience, previous supervision, and coursework that is leading to or has resulted in a degree that legitimates the therapist to practice psychotherapy. The subject of this chapter is the relationship of coursework to a supervisory relationship. Coursework can profoundly shape the way the therapist approaches both therapy and supervision. The influence of a charismatic professor can also shape the supervisory experience beyond the delivery of content of the course to inspire and shape therapists' attitudes, motivations, and approaches to learning, contributing to a more enriching and impactful educational experience. Coursework must, therefore, be understood by the supervisor and incorporated into supervision. Whether the therapist is currently enrolled in a graduate program or has completed one, the supervisor must understand what the therapist is learning or has learned from coursework and how this knowledge shapes their views and preferences for how therapy should be conducted.

Coursework can transcend a preference for a particular model. For example, a course in development adds texture to the way a model might contextualize a developmental issue such as a child's refusal to attend school. A course on addictions provides depth to the understanding of a presenting problem of an addictive nature.

When a therapist prefers a specific therapy model, the supervisor can use the therapist's curriculum to expand their clinical perspective. The curriculum is much broader than a model. Supposedly, the curriculum is or was an important component of the therapist's education. Using the knowledge from the curriculum enhances the therapist's perspective about a case and shifts the focus away from simply viewing the case from the perspective of the therapist's preferred model. For example, in all mental health programs, students take a course usually called psychopathology. This course introduces students to DSM-5-TR and the most common diagnostic categories and their presentation for the affected client. Any diagnosis opens an array

DOI: 10.4324/9781003146841-7

of questions that make the case more systemic and point toward a need for integration.

For example, if one spouse of a couple has bipolar disorder, some of the questions a supervisor might pose are: Does the client accept their diagnosis? Is the client properly medicated? Does the spouse understand the disorder? Is the spouse supportive? How does distress tolerance and affect regulation impact the way the couple have conflict? (This is part of the problem sequence.)

Each mental health profession requires a curriculum of courses to be completed as part of the degree-granting process. For each profession, required content exists in the form of theory and practices associated with the professional degree being granted. These are referred to as core competencies. Graduate programs that offer a degree in any mental health profession are afforded leeway by the accrediting body to package the core competencies however they wish through creating a curriculum consisting of requisite courses.

A limited number of graduate programs heavily emphasize systems theory, but only a few emphasize integrative practice. Therefore, an IST supervisor must provide a translation between what the therapist has learned and what comprises a systemic and integrative practice. Still, a graduate of any program can move toward and even embrace both systemic and integrative practice. As an example of a systemic and integrative curriculum, this chapter will use a curriculum developed by the creators of IST in the context of a graduate program in Marriage and Family Therapy.

Supervising Therapists Across Mental Health Professions

The methodologies and the knowledge that the therapist brings to supervision—that is, the content asset—are specified by the accreditation standards for each of the mental health professions. These standards require careful attention to how programs support the development of the core competencies of the profession and form the basis for the curriculum design and the content taught in an academic setting. For the marriage and family therapy (MFT) profession, for example, the Commission on Accreditation of Marriage and Family Therapy Education (COAMFTE) specifies five Developmental Competency Components for the development of a marriage and family therapist. Each university and accredited program has flexibility in addressing COAMFTE's competency requirements within the various courses of their curriculum (Nelson & Graves, 2011). Because MFT curricula are designed to be systemic, we will use them as a prototype for discussing curricula of other professions. A main challenge for IST supervisors is to locate systemic content within the curricula.

There are two ways in which an MFT curriculum can be designed and taught. Each way will provide opportunities and challenges for an IST supervisor who conducts supervision for therapists on their systemic and integrative therapeutic skills.

The first way and the gold standard for a systemic and integrative curriculum design is to construct every course with the IST pillars, essence, blueprint, and metaframeworks in mind. The curriculum of the Master of Science in Marriage and Family Therapy (MSMFT) program at The Family Institute at Northwestern University has been developed over the past 30 years in a way that covers the Developmental Competency Components prescribed by COAMFTE while focusing on systemic and integrative practice. In such programs, an IST supervisor knows that therapists are learning an integrative approach in their coursework, so supervision can focus on refining the application of integrative methods to client systems.

A second way of designing an MFT curriculum is to emphasize the major theories and models of the field and carefully incorporate the COAMFTE's Developmental Competency Components without providing a comprehensive integrative perspective. In this case, IST supervisors must have an awareness of how the coursework lays out and help therapists import the course content into IST formulations of their cases. The IST supervisor repackages the coursework and models of therapy within an IST framework. This skillset and the act of repackaging the content within IST's essence, blueprint, hypothesizing metaframeworks, and planning metaframeworks provides a lens for the therapist to connect to coursework and core competencies to IST, and the supervisor can meet the developmental needs specified by the MFT profession.

Vignette of a Supervisor in an IST-oriented Graduate Program

Olivia, a second-generation Latina therapist, is a seasoned clinician with five years of postgraduation supervision experience as a group and individual supervisor. Olivia's work week starts by heading to her local university to meet with her weekly supervision group. Olivia loves working with first-year MFT therapists for three hours. Today was fulfilling, supervising a clinical case with one therapist who works with an African American family of three (mother, father, and one elementary school male). The child, the identified patient, tripped down a set of stairs and broke his ankle, and now that it has healed, refuses to go back to school. The therapist requested consultation in supervision to develop a solution sequence containing an intervention. Olivia conceptualized interventions on two supervisory system levels: the supervisor–therapist and the therapist–family level. The therapist learned about solution sequences in the first quarter of their "Basic Concepts of Systems Therapy" class and was introduced to exposure strategies in their "Methods of Systems Therapy" class of their second quarter. Olivia provided feedback on the therapist's description of the avoidant interpersonal sequence and fearful intrapsychic sequence. She proposed a strategy to reduce the child's fear through gradual exposure to school, creating a hierarchy of fears list, and controlled exposure sessions to get the child to take the first step to attend school. The therapist was encouraged to collaborate with the whole family system to implement the solution sequence. Olivia felt good about the feedback from the therapist since exposure therapy was included in a course curriculum, and the therapist was confident they had the knowledge and psychological tools to implement the exposure intervention.

Vignette of an IST Supervisor with a Licensed Clinical Social Worker

In a different supervision session, Olivia met with an individual therapist, Tamyra, a licensed social worker (LCSW). Tamyra heard about systems and integrative therapy from colleagues at a private practice and sought out Olivia for her systemic clinical expertise. Tamyra recently attended an Internal Family Systems (IFS) training course and was excited about applying these clinical skills to her cases. Tamyra consulted with Olivia about a mixed-race, cisgender, heterosexual couple with the presenting problem of "poor communication." The couple reported that their arguments and conflicts started in the evenings, usually after one or both consumed alcohol. Tamyra's initial questions and statements of concern about the alcohol and arguments did not have an impact. Olivia hypothesized that alcohol constrained the couple from resolving conflict and recommended using motivational interviewing to explore this constraint with the clients. In a subsequent supervisory session, upon hearing that the motivational interviewing did not have a sufficient impact, Olivia initiated a discussion of an IFS to the conceptualization of the case, hypothesizing that alcohol served as a "firefighter" activity for one or both partners. On the basis of the IFS hypothesis, Olivia proposed an intervention that emphasized accessing self-energy. In this self-to-part relationship, each client can bring the self to the conversation so that they could self-regulate and create a safe space to discuss and find a way to repair conflict. Tamyra had previously taken a course on treating addiction that focused on detoxification and the use of medical-assisted therapies for substance use. Olivia introduced a systemic hypothesis for addressing communication issues and substance use disorders, expanding Tamyra's understanding and experience from a solely medical model approach to a broader systemic approach.

Olivia hypothesized on the clinical cases at the supervisor–therapist and supervisor–client level, and her supervisory feedback was based on the therapist's level of training and knowledge, keeping the clinical recommendations consistent with the therapist's experience.

In both these supervision consultations, knowledge of the graduate and, in the second example, postgraduate coursework is a vital asset for the direct supervision system since it acts as a basis for the supervisor to provide developmental recommendations in a manner that is consistent with the therapist's experience and simultaneously considers effective treatment planning strategies for the client who is in the indirect supervisory system.

In the context of her involvement in the IST-oriented graduate program, Olivia recently substituted for a second-year group supervisor on maternity leave for three months. The therapists were entering their second semester of the second year in the Marriage and Family Therapy graduate program. Olivia reviewed the syllabi of the therapists' most recent courses, one of which is an advanced course on Intimate Relations. Samantha, one of the therapists, presented a couple's case, where the presenting problem was communication difficulties and inability to resolve conflict. The joint goal of the client was to de-escalate conflict and navigate relational differences without causing distress to their children. Using the blueprint of IST, Samantha shared a preliminary hypothesis that one partner had more access to resources, influence, and worked outside the home, giving them freedom to navigate home and work responsibilities at their sole discretion. When the couple tried to rebalance the resources and needs, this frequently led to anger and polarization. Samantha enacted a solution sequence in the recent therapy session, and the feedback revealed the failed attempts at listening due to defensiveness and hostile criticism. Later in the session, Samantha requested more information about the respective spouses' families of origin experiences with conflict. Samantha learned that one partner's mom was critical and controlling. The other partner grew up in a home where the father had an addiction. Samantha mapped the interpersonal and intrapsychic sequences and tried multiple interventions, including speaker–listener, enactment, and strategies from integrative behavioral therapy. Despite the attempts to intervene in the system, the conflict persisted, and each spouse rigidly held onto their defensive ways of talking and hostile criticism of one another.

Olivia, having familiarity with the content and method of integrative thinking in the Intimate Relations course syllabus, praised Samantha for her curiosity and for her level of integrative thinking that was becoming more expansive and complex. Olivia helped Samantha consider the bottom of the matrix hypothesis and intervention as they realized that both clients' reactivity was deeply rooted in the past. Olivia's hypothesis expanded to attachment injuries. Olivia connected the poor communication and conflict resolution style rooted to their early life experiences. The couple's struggles to feel safe, seen, and heard were addressed and their reactivity was dramatically reduced.

To think integratively, Olivia first helped Samantha attend to the constraints at the top of the IST matrix, where she recommended communication and active listening skills for managing client conflict. She demonstrated how to help the client implement and practice these skills, so that the therapist can successfully contain the conflict. Olivia read the feedback and hypothesized that Samantha needed to do more in session. Olivia recommended that Samantha expand her conceptualization of the sequence by applying the vulnerability cycle (Scheinkman & Fishbane, 2004), identifying the clients' survival strategies and connecting this to their early life vulnerability, with the goal to help the clients soften and connect with each other's primary emotions. There were moments of softness, but the clients returned to their homeostatic maladaptive communication pattern. In subsequent supervision sessions, Olivia hypothesized and identified constraints of early attachment injuries that would constrain how they made meaning of experiences (M1 level of the mind constraints). Olivia expanded her hypothesis to the M2 level of the mind, which identifies how the organization of the mind constrains the clients from overcoming conflict. She then connected the hypothesis and interventions with intergenerational hypothesis and intrapsychic conceptualization.

Olivia recognized that the therapists had learned the failure-driven concepts of integration and then borrowed strategies from Internal Family Systems (M2 level of mind). The client's survival strategies and vulnerability (M1 level of mind) were conceptually linked to managers and exiles from the Internal Family Systems therapy model. The therapists intervened with the client's manager parts and helped the client unburden their early attachment wounds (exiles). This enabled the client to bring self-energy, and the couple was able to soften addressing conflict in a collaborative, resolutive way.

Curriculum Design and Integration

Olivia's approach to consultation and applying integrative thinking is deeply rooted in IST, which has a series of guidelines and a storehouse of theories available to the systemic supervisor. These supervisory tools include the blueprint, the essence diagram, hypothesizing and planning metaframeworks that facilitate case conceptualization and problem resolution in simple, straightforward ways that solve problems with a few constraints, yet are easily able to expand to more complex problem-solving depending on the severity and complexity of constraints.

To apply problem resolution strategies and supervise clinical cases, IST has a necessarily complex integration methodology. Olivia can case conceptualize and provide feedback to the therapist in a systemic and integrative way. The therapist already knows this integration approach and needs further supervision on applying more sophisticated integrative thinking skills to their cases.

Any professional body or educational institution planning to meet integrative core competencies should include theories and integration methods in its curriculum. Without specifying and teaching an approach to integration or where the integration methodology of the therapist's curriculum differs from a supervisor's experience, the supervisor is tasked with performing a dual role of case consultation and the role of teacher, increasing the complexity in the supervision process.

IST Integration Strategies Included in Curriculum Design

Learning intervention methods and integration strategies cannot be fully absorbed in supervision alone. The development of a systemic therapist requires the principles of systemic integration to be included in the course syllabi. Teaching IST integration using a specific method of integration principles and theory provides the intellectual scaffolding from which a student begins to develop into a systemic and integrative therapist. Supervisors then deepen the learning experience by providing case consultation and help translate the knowledge into clinical application. This dual role of course instructor and supervisor is split to enhance the developmental experience of the therapist in training.

Over the past three decades, the field of psychotherapy has been flooded with numerous empirically validated and research-informed treatments for specific client disorders and presenting problems, as well as for specific populations. Psychotherapy programs at various educational institutions have used different methods to integrate empirically validated treatment models into their curricula (Beck et al., 2014). Therapists must assimilate this information and understand the clinical, theoretical, and systemic implications when they apply an empirically informed intervention to their clinical cases. Supervisors must broaden their own understanding of the empirical treatment methods and learn specific supervision skills while considering the empirical treatments therapists bring to their clinical work. This creates an increased level of integrative complexity in the supervisory system.

Integration has a long history in couples and family therapy. Lebow (1984) highlighted the importance of integrative therapy and the unique contribution of integration to couples and family therapy. For the past five decades, well-known integrative family therapy strategies have been developed, and simultaneously, methods of integration emerged that include common factors, technical eclecticism, common factors of integration, theoretical integration, stages of change model, and others that integrate interventions into the clinical decision-making process. This level of complexity historically posed unique challenges in the supervisory context, and the teaching of integrative skills was primarily relegated to the supervisor.

The spirit and philosophy of IST is operationalized by the planning matrix. It codifies the many interventions, strategies, and integration principles created in the field of psychotherapy. The planning matrix holds the six categories of strategies and interventions decontextualized from the models of psychotherapy from which they originated. This decontextualized process involves borrowing interventions from the different models of therapy and classifying these interventions according to a common goal. IST then includes these strategies in the different planning metaframeworks irrespective of the entire model from which they came. For example, exposure is an intervention primarily discussed in cognitive behavioral therapy and borrowed from the behavioral psychotherapist (Wolpe, 1961). The planning matrix assumes that all therapists engage in exposure, a common strategy. For example, a therapist uses exposure to help a client face their fears—that is, secondary emotions—which is also a form of exposure practice.

The planning matrix, therefore, is a storehouse of interventions that operate independently of the model from which they came. This decontextualization principle is closely associated with the theoretical eclecticism integration method of Fraenkel & Pinsof (2001).

The Planning Matrix and Integration

IST organizes and integrates the different models of psychotherapy into six planning metaframeworks and three intervention contexts that form 18 cells of the matrix (see Figure 1.3). The planning metaframeworks and the matrix meet the requirement of one or more MFT core competencies for interventions and systemic integration.

The first of the planning metaframeworks depicted in the first row and cell in the matrix is the action planning metaframework. This planning metaframework borrows strategies from all action-oriented models such as structural, behavioral, and strategic models of therapy. These therapy models focus primarily on behavior and action as a method of change and problem resolution. For example, when working with a high-conflict couple, we can use an enactment strategy with a speaker–listener intervention to help resolve the rigid communication boundary and soften conflict. This strategy and details of the intervention can be found in the action strategy at the family level, which is the first cell of the matrix.

The first three planning meta frameworks, action, emotion/meaning, and biobehavioral, share a here-and-now temporal orientation and are concerned with the client's current functioning. They draw on problem formation, maintenance, and resolution theories, and aim to change behavioral, experiential, and biological constraints. The last three planning metaframeworks deal with the family of origin, internal representation, and self. They target then-and-there strategies.

The guidelines for IST provide a set of principles for the application of the matrix strategies and interventions within a clinical context. The guidelines for choosing systemic strategies and integration methods recommend that problem-solving therapy starts with the family or couple's context (interpersonal guideline) and focuses on brief interventions early in treatment that explicitly lift current constraints to problem resolution (cost-effective and temporal guidelines). Once a clinician intervenes with strategies from the cells in the first three planning metaframeworks and reads the feedback when these strategies fail, they can move to the next set of cells and select strategies that focus on historical or past constraints (failure-driven guidelines), all the way down the matrix to past constraints at an individual level. The constraints guide us where to land on the planning metaframeworks, and the failure-driven guideline provides theoretical guidance to move down the matrix in a collaborative, flexible approach to problem resolution without rigid progression.

For example, Olivia first conceptualized with the therapist about the clinical case, recommended interventions from the vulnerability cycle, and suggested the method of softening by accessing the primary emotions. In the follow-up consultation, the therapist, on reading the feedback, hypothesized the clients were unable to share their vulnerability. Using the failure-driven guideline, Olivia suggested the therapist try a "parts" intervention from Internal Family Systems theory, which is a historical strategy situated in the fourth level of the matrix.

The planning matrix holds the strategies decontextualized from therapy models and could be applicable at the different stages of the therapeutic process. The planning matrix itself does not specify specific strategies for a clinical session. Rather, strategies are chosen from the context of therapy. Any graduate program or curriculum in each accrediting professional body can create its own planning matrix. The course content should include the systemic domain focus (individual, couple, family) and the temporal focus (in-session, here-and-now, recent remote, past) (Pinsof et al., 2011). The strategies for problem resolution should be selected with specific techniques nested within each strategy (e.g., for the exposure intervention, the strategies can include, but are not limited to, in-vivo, imaginal, and single exposure; to aversive stimuli and managing the fear response). This is an example of when exposure is the intervention, and "single exposure" is the "strategy."

This integration method is helpful for therapists who will be exposed through coursework to the program's preferred set of strategies and interventions. Supervisors can use the matrix to illustrate integration, demonstrating to therapists how to work with a client system when interventions have failed, thus rendering the therapist unsure of how to proceed with the case.

Olivia, a seasoned supervisor familiar with the IST integration method, would be able to hypothesize and intervene along with the therapist from many disciplines of psychotherapy. This skill set would flow naturally as she uncovered different client system constraints presented by her therapists. Regardless of treatment strategies, systemic integration aims to expand our awareness of the whole person and family system.

Integrative Curriculum Design

Fraenkel and Pinsof (2001) explained the recursive curriculum design method developed and refined over the past 30 years at The Family Institute. Therapists are first introduced to a broad metatheory, the IST framework.

This starts with a general introduction in the first quarter while simultaneously acknowledging that it is impossible to master all the theories that the IST metamodel borrows from psychotherapy.

In the second quarter, the therapists learn how to integrate basic interventions into their early work with clients. In the third quarter, they study a variety of models of therapy, with a specific focus on family therapy models, so that they have a good enough understanding of fundamental theories and interventions. This "Family Therapy Treatment Models" course is a way to build knowledge about the field of couples and family therapy. Concurrent with and following these early courses, the therapists are exposed to IST material within each course throughout the two years, "progressively going into more depth with each presentation and application" (Fraenkel and Pinsof, 2001, p.76). Therapists start their internship experience at the end of their first quarter of the first year. This method of curriculum design and phased delivery builds a foundation, and then contributes to the therapists' clinical competency early in a graduate program.

Exploring the Integrative Components of a Master's in Marriage and Family Therapy Curriculum

To provide more detail regarding a curriculum that reflects IST practice, the following discussion of the curriculum used in the Master of Science in Marriage and Family Therapy at Northwestern University includes the following: (1) a listing of the course title of the entire curriculum; (2) a presentation of five courses that are central to learning IST.

While the Northwestern curriculum is COAMFTE-approved, it differs from some MFT curricula in a significant way. Because IST is a perspective suited to the practice of family, couple, and individual therapy, the curriculum exposes students to courses needed to practice not only family therapy but also individual and couple therapy. This design not only reflects the practice of IST, but it also reflects the reality of what MFT therapists do in their practices. Although this curriculum is up to date, its design and content provide a solid foundation that can be easily adapted and updated to meet future needs. Lorås et al. (2023) and Whittaker et al. (2023) have shown that MFT's caseloads are made up of at least 50 percent individuals. Moreover, whereas couple therapy was once considered to be a part of family therapy, in the past two decades it has emerged as a distinct specialty with its own models and literature.

Curriculum Design to Support Integration and Supervision

This is a suggested curriculum for the MSMFT program that satisfies COAMFTE's Developmental Competency Components:

First Quarter:

- MSFT 401-0 Basic Concepts of Systems Therapy
- MSFT 421-0 Systemic Assessment
- MSFT 428-0 Legal, Ethical, and Professional Issues in Marriage and Family Therapy
- MSFT 480-0 Pre-Practicum in Marriage and Family Therapy

Second Quarter:

- MSFT 402-0 Methods of Systems Therapy
- MSFT 410-0 Human Development
- MSFT 430-0 Power, Privilege, and Difference: Practicing Cultural Curiosity and Humility in a Multicultural World
- MSFT 481-0 Internship in Marriage and Family Therapy

Third Quarter:

- MSFT 403-0 Self and Systems: Theory and Application
- MSFT 411-0 Intimate Relations I
- MSFT 436-0 Family Therapy Treatment Models
- MSFT 481-0 Internship in Marriage and Family Therapy

Fourth Quarter:

- MSFT 424-0 Group Therapy
- MSFT 437-0 Family Therapy with Children and Adolescents
- MSFT 481-0 Internship in Marriage and Family Therapy

Fifth Quarter

- MSFT 413-0 Intimate Relations II
- MSFT 422-0 Family Research
- MSFT 481-0 Internship in Marriage and Family Therapy

Sixth Quarter

- MSFT 427-0 Family of Origin: Systemic Perspectives on Risk and Resilience
- MSFT 440-0 Systemic Perspectives in the Treatment of Substance Use/Misuse and Addiction
- MSFT 495-0 Capstone Project
- MSFT 481-0 Internship in Marriage and Family Therapy

Seventh Quarter;

- MSFT 429-0 Sex Therapy
- MSFT 412-0 Special Problems and Populations
- MSFT 495-0 Capstone Project
- MSFT 481-0 Internship in Marriage and Family Therapy

We have selected and expanded on five courses from the COAMFTE-approved curriculum for the following reasons:

- The courses and curriculum, which are updated annually, have been evaluated by the authors against the integrative and systemic courses taught at the MSMFT program from the past decade. They recommend this as a model for future course content.
- Where a graduate psychology program is trying to shape their educational and supervision curriculum to be more IST informed, we recommend including the two foundational courses which are the "Basic Concepts of Systems Therapy" and "Methods of Systems Therapy" in their curriculum.
- Two-year MFT curriculum includes courses beyond the immediate scope of family therapy models. The inclusion of these non-traditional courses is pivotal for cultivating a nuanced understanding of systemic theory and its integration, preparing both supervisors and therapists for a more nuanced grasp of therapeutic practices and steering them toward becoming therapists and supervisors informed by Integrative Systemic Therapy (IST). Specifically, courses like "Family Therapy Treatment Models" and "Family of Origin: Systemic Perspectives on Risk and Resilience" are integral, as they are the secondary framework necessary for fostering the move towards becoming more IST informed in the therapeutic work.
- Family therapy programs are deeply entrenched in family therapy methodologies, often overlooking or paying limited attention to the specific needs of individual therapy. In contrast, the MFT course curriculum uniquely addresses this gap by including a "Self and Systems" course. This course bridges the divide, ensuring that practitioners and supervisors are well-equipped to treat individuals and relational cases, thereby broadening their clinical competency integrating models of therapy beyond the traditional relational focus of family therapy.

First Quarter: "Basic Concepts of Systems Therapy"

Our approach to teaching systemic therapy and integration begins in the first fall quarter of the two-year graduate program. The syllabus design for the "Basic Concepts of Systems Therapy" course was created by William Russell (2022) and the course objectives and learning outcomes are described below.

"Basic Concepts of Systems Therapy" is the first course to introduce therapists to systemic therapy's theoretical underpinnings and provide an integrative framework for assessment and intervention in human problems. The course establishes the conceptual foundation for the MSMFT program's mission of educating therapists as knowledgeable, competent, systemic, culturally sensitive, and empirically informed marriage and family therapists (Russell, 2022).

Particular attention will be given to the pillars, concepts, metaframe-works, and clinical guidelines of the Integrative Systemic Therapy (IST) model. This approach provides a set of constructs for planning and conducting therapy, a structure for containing and organizing the body of knowledge associated with MFT, and a basis for lifelong professional learning and growth. Class format will include didactic presentations, clinical case examples, and video illustrations; discussion of readings and class material; and application to clinical work and professional development.

A key outcome of the course is the establishment of a foundational knowledge base and the introduction of a perspective for integrating concepts, models, and techniques. Therapists will theoretically understand the essence diagram and blueprint diagram of IST. The course also addresses cultural sensitivity and respect for diversity through the recurring theme of culture in the integrative perspective (IST), a three-hour block devoted to cultural context material (the Culture Metaframework) (Russell, 2022).

At any time in a supervision session, a systemic supervisor should ask the therapist, "What are you working on now?" To answer this question in their first semester, the therapist in training should be able to point to an essence diagram and conceptualize where they land in the therapeutic process with the client. Therapists should be familiar with the terminology and concepts shared by the supervisor and able to receive and assimilate feedback due to the common language of the therapeutic process established in the Basics of Concepts of Systemic Therapy coursework.

Second Quarter: "Methods of Systems Therapy"

The second course in the series—"Methods of Systems Theory"—is scheduled to build on previous systemic and integrative knowledge. This course is sequenced with an emphasis on shifting the learning experience from acquiring clinical principles to the practical application of the theory over the previous semester (Venketramen, 2024). This course is a companion to "Basic Concepts in Systems Therapy" and "Family Therapy Treatment Models."

The instruction is focused on teaching strategies from different models of therapy that have been decontextualized from their models and which therapists can apply to their clinical cases without needing to be an expert in the model of therapy from which the strategy is borrowed.

Having been introduced to IST in the first quarter, this course continues to solidify the use of IST in therapy. Following an overview of the practice components of IST, therapists will be introduced to the "common factors" of therapy. The balance of the course will use the "module" format to introduce therapists to a set of the most valuable strategies and methods of systemic therapy. Therapists will learn the method, demonstrate it, and practice it themselves. At the end of the module, all clinicians should become familiar with the tools and ways to apply these strategies in clinical cases.

The methods content and course design introduce therapists to embrace the failure-driven approach by trying strategies, reading the feedback, using the hypothesizing metaframeworks to identify constraints, and move down the matrix thoughtfully and methodologically so that they can adapt to building "good enough" experience and intervene at a "good enough" level.

Course outline:

- Week 1: A detailed exploration of the interpersonal and intrapsychic sequences of the IST approach to therapy.
- Week 2: Exploration of structural family therapy and understanding transactional patterns in client systems, including the enactment strategy.
- Week 3: Strategy of cognitive restructuring and exposure strategies.
- Week 4: Host a sequences lab where therapists role-play and gain practical experience with identifying internal and external sequences, deepening their practical skills in uncovering problem sequences, and developing solutions sequences.
- Week 5: Common factors of therapy.
- Week 6: Narrative therapy including externalization and meaning-making.
- Week 7: Action-focused method working processing emotions.
- Week 8: Conversing with circular questioning.
- Weeks 9/10: Experiential exercises, including integration strategies supported by IST directly from the planning matrix.

The culture and gender metaframeworks are routinely opened for every one of the methods taught in the course and are seen as part of the entire coursework (Venketramen, 2024).

Therapists will develop clinical expertise in working with higher-level constructs of psychotherapy strategies and learn how to apply this strategy in a failure-driven way to apply the planning metaframeworks of IST.

Building on this course, supervisors can shift to helping therapists broaden their skill set to sequentialize problems at the interpersonal and intrapsychic levels and help therapists shift their thinking to applying systemic strategies to their casework. Therapists will seek consultation on applying various clinical strategies and deepen their experience with assessment and intervention in the clinical session.

Third Quarter: "Family Therapy Treatment Models"

The third recursive step in integrative theory learning requires the knowledge of various models of psychotherapy integrated in a manner that aligns with multiple cells in the planning matrix. The course description and course content were designed and authored by Zavada (2023).

"Course Description: This course examines the major treatment models that have emerged throughout the development of systemic therapy, including their respective philosophical underpinnings, theories, assessments, and interventions nested within them" (Zavada, 2023).

In addition, the course also explores how to use the models' strategies to navigate IST's Planning Matrix.

Course content: The course will address the following systemic and family therapy models: Structural Family Therapy, Bowen Family Systems Theory, Contextual Family Therapy, Satir's Human Growth Model, Strategic Family Therapy, Solution-Focused Brief Systems Therapy (SFBT), Narrative Family Therapy, Internal Family Systems (IFS), integration between the models of therapy based on the planning matrix (Zavada, 2023).

Outcomes: Therapists will be able to (a) recognize the critical figures of different models and their contributions to the field, (b) describe key concepts and interventions of the different family therapy models, and (c) discuss how each theory understands family dynamics, health, and symptoms (Zavada, 2023).

We sequenced this course to follow the Basic Concepts of Systems Theory and Methods course in order to bridge the gap in the level of theoretical knowledge with all therapists, irrespective of their undergraduate background and level of experience. Therapists must also explore how each model addresses diversity and cultural sensitivity.

Rather than the approach of "teach a model of the week," we recommend that this course be taught integratively, matching the strategies of the models to the cells of the IST matrix.

Once therapists have understood the family therapy models, they are ready to match interventions that lift constraints and apply these interventions directly to the clinical cases. Supervisors can hypothesize and recommend interventions directly from the list of models specified in the basics course. Supervisors can read the video feedback and share feedback on ways to increase skill and experience with a particular intervention strategy.

Sixth Quarter: "Family of Origin"

This course curriculum that was developed to follow from the IST meta-models was formulated by Dr. Nancy Burgoyne in 2016. The course aims to help the therapist understand and explore two questions: "What makes for a 'good enough' family of origin?" and "What options do adult children have for responding to issues nested at this layer of the interpersonal and intrapsychic system?" (Burgoyne, 2016).

The course is designed to view this question from several angles. The coursework will consider what Intergenerational Family Therapists contribute to understanding family of origin. Next, the course will consider an Object Relations Theory perspective, which provides a framework for thinking systemically about the intra-psychic world and the impact of a person's history on their functioning. Finally, the course will integrate an empirically informed, strength-based resilience framework to identify key family processes that support adaptive functioning in adversity. Therapists will be asked to engage in an ongoing dialectical process between these variables to develop a complex, integrated perspective on Family of Origin.

(Burgoyne, 2016)

Course objectives and therapist learning outcomes:

Therapists completing this course will (1) understand and be able to articulate the ways Family of Origin has been considered generally in the field of Family Therapy; (2) develop a beginning level of understanding of how the intra-psychic system develops according to Object Relations Theory (a) through developmental stages (b) through internalized relationships; (3) critically evaluate the veracity of Object Relations Theory, and deterministic theoretical models to predict functioning, based on empirical evidence; (4) understand and be able to articulate the ways Family of Origin would be considered and addressed within the IST framework.

Intergenerational models will be the primary focus of this course. This will include Bowenian Family Therapy, Family of Origin Therapy as conceptualized by James Framo, and Boszormenyi-Nagy's Contextual Therapy. There will be a detailed exploration of the development of intra-psychic functioning: Object Relations. The syllabus will include differentiation and dialogue in intergenerational relationships; shame & worthiness: An exploration through the lens of culture and gender, affect and Mood Regulation, the sequelae of multi-stressed families.

(Burgoyne, 2016)

The IST integration principles included in the planning matrix consider the family of origin metaframework and theories as a "swing" metaframework. The failure-driven approach to interventions leads us to consider interventions with the family of origin prior to engaging in deep intrapsychic Self and systems work.

When following the course content, the supervision process can (1) provide therapists with a theoretically grounded, empirically informed, strength-based framework for conceptualizing family of origin and (2) provide theoretically consistent options for responding therapeutically to constraints nested at this level of the system.

Third Quarter: "Self and Other Systems"

The coursework and description are from a historical curriculum presented by Dr. Nancy Burgoyne (2015). The task in this course is to pose questions asked by every philosophical, religious, and social science tradition: What is the Self? How is it created and manifested? What does it mean for human beings and their relationships? The vast literature on the concept of Self speaks to its importance and difficulty in defining it. The goals will be to (1) explore perspectives relevant to the task of becoming a family therapist; (2) deepen understanding of the reciprocal effects of the Self and the systems with which it interacts; (3) consider the application of these ideas to the process of conducting therapy; (4) place our emergent understanding of the Self into the context of IST framework (Burgoyne, 2015).

Course objectives:

> Therapists completing this course will (1) understand and be able to articulate the ways Self has been considered generally in the field of Family Therapy (2) understand and be able to articulate the ways Self has been explicitly considered within the TFI Perspective (3) understand and be able to articulate the value of considering the Self at each juncture in the Blueprint for Therapy, (4) develop and be able to articulate how the ideas developed in the class would be applied clinically, and (5) develop a nascent understanding of what the Self is and why it is relevant to human development and psychotherapy.
>
> This course covers early family therapy approaches, specifically structural and strategic models of conceptualization of the Self, focusing on individual internal experiences. It delves into neurobiology's role in shaping the Self and examines how temperament affects family systems. The course explores attachment theory and its impact on Self and family dynamics. Therapists will learn about the Internal Family Systems model. They will develop an explicit understanding of how this model, nested within the mind meta-framework, contributes to the IST perspective on Self and mind with an explicit focus on the spiritual premise of Self. The concept of self-differentiation and the role of Selves in relationships are vital topics. Additionally, the course addresses narrative family therapy's approach to the Self and will focus on the impact of trauma on the Self and the development of the internal system. Finally, there will be an elementary understanding of the contribution of Object Relations Theory and Self Psychology to the understanding of Self, with a broad introduction to the work of Heinz Cohort. Therapists will develop an explicit understanding of how this model contributes to the IST perspective on Self and Mind.
>
> (Burgoyne, 2015)

Supervisors can conceptualize cases using self and systems theory and an area for bringing specialists from the indirect therapist system to be part of the direct system. When it is clinically relevant, we recommend for a supervisor to advise the therapist to refer clients for specialist treatment—for example, referring a client diagnosed with borderline personality disorder to meet with a Dialectical Behavioral therapist to work on emotion regulation or refer the client to therapist for deep intrapsychic Self work.

Capstone – Sixth and Seventh Quarters

The MSMFT program at Northwestern University provides students with the opportunity to synthesize the knowledge and experience they gained in the program through completion of a capstone experience. In this sense, the students' journey of learning culminates in the capstone course, in which they demonstrate their ability to construct an integrative and systemic formulation of a case as well as their attainment of specific IST skills. The capstone instructor provides evaluative and instructive feedback on their work.

The capstone consists of three elements: a case conceptualization paper, a formal case presentation, and the submission of video recordings that demonstrate key IST skills.

Case Conceptualization Paper

This paper requires students to tell the story of a case. It includes a discussion of assessment and treatment as well as how the student navigated the problem-solving steps of the IST essence. Using the IST perspective to break down a case, students explore the problems presented by the clients, the solutions identified, and the application of therapy techniques. This assignment provides the opportunity for the student to demonstrate that they connect theory with practice, think critically, and use feedback effectively. It also requires the student to illustrate cultural sensitivity and understanding of principles of ethical practice.

Formal Case Presentation

Students present an active clinical case to their supervision group and supervisors. Students present for 30 minutes, including two short video clips from their therapy sessions, followed by a discussion. This process demonstrates that students have learned to present cases from a systemic and integrative perspective, and receive and incorporate feedback from peers and supervisors.

Submission of Skill Demonstration Video Recordings

Students submit video recordings of their therapy sessions that demonstrate key IST skills. They must demonstrate that they have acquired key skills such as building a therapeutic alliance, identifying problem sequences and solutions, identifying constraints, and applying specific interventions to address constraints.

The course instructor reviews the three elements of the capstone and provides detailed feedback on the application of the essence and blueprint of IST to clinical work. This course is essential to the program as it consolidates learning, evaluates the students' progress, and further prepares them for real-world therapy situations.

Conclusion

This chapter has explored the role of a program curriculum in shaping the beliefs and practices of therapists whether they are in training or have graduated. The systemic competencies across the four licensure-eligible clinical fields of study have been explored. The MFT degree and its competency domains are emphasized because this degree is considered to have the most systematically formulated course objectives and proposed systemic curricula. These curricula are designed to align with the therapist's learning sequences, fostering a congruence that enhances systemic clinical supervision. In this context, systemic supervision is emphasized as a crucial element, extending beyond mere oversight to include the psychological foundation theory as part of the supervision of clinical cases. Such supervision is pivotal in ensuring that therapists grasp theoretical knowledge and apply this theory in their clinical practices. The curriculum emerges as a vital supervisory tool, with its design reflecting a degree of isomorphism with the supervisory process, reinforcing the application of theory in clinical settings. Educational programs dedicated to offering comprehensive education and field practicum clinical supervision with a systemic training focus are encouraged to adopt these recommendations within their course development strategies.

References

Beck, J. G., Castonguay, L. G., Chronis-Tuscano, A., Klonsky, E. D., McGinn, L. K., & Youngstrom, E. A. (2014). Principles for training in evidence-based psychology: Recommendations for the graduate curricula in clinical psychology. *Clinical Psychology: Science and Practice*, 21(4), 410–424. https://doi.org/10.1111/cpsp.12079.

Burgoyne, N. (2016). Bottom of the Matrix Intervening [Unpublished manuscript].

Burgoyne, N. (2016). MSFT 427 Family of Origin: Systemic Perspective on Risk and Resilience [Syllabus]. Center for Applied Psychological and Family Studies, Northwestern University.

Burgoyne, N. (2015). MSFT 403—Self and Other Systems [Syllabus]. Center for Applied Psychological and Family Studies, Northwestern University.

Fraenkel, P., & Pinsof, W. M. (2001). Teaching family therapy-centered integration: Assimilation and beyond. *Journal of Psychotherapy Integration*, 11(1), 59–85. https://doi.org/10.1023/A:1026629024866.

Lebow, J. L. (1984). On the value of integrating approaches to family therapy. *Journal of Marital and Family Therapy*, 10(2), 127–138. https://doi.org/10.1111/j.1752-0606.1984.tb00003.x.

Lorås, L., Whittaker, K., Stokkebekk, J., & Tilden, T. (2023). Researching what we practice—The paradigm of systemic family research: Part 1. *Family Process*, 62(3), 947–960. https://doi.org/10.1111/famp.12903.

Nelson, T. S., & Graves, T. (2011). Core competencies in advanced training: What supervisors say about graduate training. *Journal of Marital and Family Therapy*, 37(4), 429–451. https://doi.org/10.1111/j.1752-0606.2010.00216.x.

Pinsof, W., Breunlin, D. C., Russell, W. P., & Lebow, J. (2011). Integrative problem-centered metaframeworks therapy II: planning, conversing, and reading feedback. *Family Process*, 50(3), 314–336. https://doi.org/10.1111/j.1545-5300.2011.01361.x.

Russell, W. (2022). MSFT 401—Family Therapy I: Basic Concepts of Systems Therapy [Syllabus]. Center for Applied Psychological and Family Studies, Northwestern University.

Russell, W. P., & Breunlin, D. C. (2019). Transcending therapy models and managing complexity: Suggestions from integrative systemic therapy. *Family Process*, 58(3), 641–655. https://doi.org/10.1111/famp.12482.

Scheinkman, M., & Fishbane, M. D. (2004). The vulnerability cycle: working with impasses in couple therapy. *Family Process*, 43(3), 279–299. https://doi.org/10.1111/j.1545-5300.2004.00023.x.

Venketramen, N (2024). MSFT 402—Methods of Systems Therapy [Syllabus]. Center for Applied Psychological and Family Studies, Northwestern University.

Whittaker, K., Stokkebekk, J., Lorås, L., & Tilden, T. (2023). Researching what we practice—The paradigm of systemic family research: Part 2. *Family Process*, 62(3), 961–975. https://doi.org/10.1111/famp.12921.

Wolpe, J. (1961). The systematic desensitization treatment of neuroses. *The Journal of Nervous and Mental Disease*, 132, 189–203. https://doi.org/10.1097/00005053-196103000-00001.

Zavada, A. (2023). MSFT 436—Family Therapy Treatment Models [Syllabus]. Center for Applied Psychological and Family Studies, Northwestern University.

Index

For Product Safety Concerns and Information please contact our EU
representative GPSR@taylorandfrancis.com
Taylor & Francis Verlag GmbH, Kaufingerstraße 24, 80331 München, Germany

www.ingramcontent.com/pod-product-compliance
Lightning Source LLC
Chambersburg PA
CBHW050609280326
41932CB00016B/2968

9 780367 705442